THE CITY GARDENER'S
Cookbook

TOTALLY FRESH, MOSTLY VEGETARIAN,
DECIDEDLY DELICIOUS RECIPES
FROM SEATTLE'S P-PATCHES

P-PATCH COOKB...

D...

Eile...

Nan...

Barbara Donnette

SASQUATCH BOOKS
SEATTLE

Printed in the United States of America.

Cover design by Kate L. Thompson
Cover illustration by Margaret Chodos-Irvine
Interior design and illustrations by Suzanne Brooker
Edited by Patricia Draher

A bold and colorful patchwork quilt was hand made by the P-Patch gardeners in commemoration of the program's 20th anniversary. Rebecca Kerber's square, one of 30, is featured on page viii. Photograph by Eduardo Calderón.

Library of Congress Cataloging in Publication Data
The City gardener's cookbook : totally fresh, mostly vegetarian, decidedly
  delicious recipes from Seattle's P-Patches / P-Patch Cookbook
  Committee, Donna Pierce . . . [et al.].
     p.   cm.
   Includes index.
   ISBN 0-912365-99-4 : $14.95
   1. Vegetarian cookery. 2. Community gardens—Washington (State)—
Seattle. I. Pierce, Donna. II. P-Patch Cookbook Committee (Seattle,
Wash.)
TX837.C485 1994
641.5'636—dc20   93-42640
                                                                  CIP

Sasquatch Books
1008 Western Avenue
Seattle, Washington 98104
(206) 467-4300

TABLE OF CONTENTS

PREFACE AND ACKNOWLEDGMENTS

Seattle's P-Patch community gardens flourish in thirty diverse neighborhoods throughout the city, bringing people together to grow vegetables, fruits, herbs, and flowers. Volunteerism, friendship, and community pride form strong roots for the program. No matter what our position in the world, each of us is transformed through the simple act of gardening side-by-side with others. As one gardener said, "Every time I visit a P-Patch I hate to leave the warm and inclusive atmosphere I encounter there. I have long felt blessed to have my own large city garden, but I now realize that a garden full of people all loving the earth and supporting each other and the community has a magic to it that a solitary gardener's plot could never have."

This collection of recipes and stories is a celebration of 20 years of P-Patch gardening in Seattle. It was inspired by the far-reaching, positive impacts of community gardening and a desire to spread the goodwill of the P-Patch Program even further. It was never our intention just to write a cookbook, but rather to introduce you, the reader, to growing and cooking the freshest organic vegetables and to encourage you to try new things, perhaps even start a garden in your own neighborhood.

We are four community gardeners who have developed this book as a fundraiser for the P-Patch Advisory Council, a nonprofit community organization in support of the City of Seattle's P-Patch Program, which resides in the Department of Housing and Human Services. Donna Pierce started it all with the idea of raising money to build more gardens for the hundreds of people on the waiting list. Her eclectic knowledge and artistic flair with both gardens and food form the essence of this book. With irrepressible enthusiasm, Donna presented dramatic five-course meals garnished with flowers and fragrant herbs to see us through the editing meetings. The indefatigable Eileen Eininger made the book manifest, organizing over 100 imaginative recipe testers and volumes of word processing. She kept the gradually evolving cookbook in retrievable folders stacked about her living room for years. She's wondering how to redecorate now. Nancy Allen was our liaison with everybody, wrote real English, and provided a voice of reason when, during late-night writing sessions, giddiness took over. Barbara Donnette wrote the delightful stories about each of the P-Patches.

The P-Patch Program represents many cultures, gardens, and people. Almost 150 of these gardeners helped us write this book. What began as a simple recipe testing project by P-Patch gardeners grew into an amazing, exciting, and often hilarious network of cooks, tasters, and flavor critics. Our testers were everywhere: Easter brunches, potlucks, dinner parties, neighborhood get-togethers, and picnics. Feedback about recipes arrived in the mail with diagrams of vegetables, songs to go with the titles, doodles, and splattered ingredients. From simple beginnings came wonderful rewards as we watched our testers become exposed to new ideas for cooking with garden produce. They began what we hope will become a parade of gardeners and cooks who will experience the joys of communal gardening and shared harvests.

Our special thanks go to Sharon Lindenau and Kris Markewitz for seemingly endless word processing; to Lisa Kadyk who, sadly for us, left the editing team for postdoctoral research in Wisconsin; and to Kathy Krogslund and her famous P-Patch Lunch Bunch testers. Thanks also to Robert Pincus, Davis McKinnon, Lauren Fortune, Blair Delaubenfels, and Richard Mattrass for help with research, interviewing, and final formatting; and to Schuyler Ingle, Anne Depue, and Patricia Draher for their encouragement.

Our thanks extend further into the P-Patch community, to the people who contributed and tested recipes, told us their stories, and provided their support: Michael Alexander, Anastasia, Vicki Artimovich, Ed Atwood, Helen Badgely, Colleen Baumgartner, Craig Berg, Mary Bicknell, Debbie Birnby, Vicki Bjorkman, Michael Boer, Karen Boyd, Phillip and Sarah Brazeau, Diane Brooks, Julie Brown, Mary Burki, Joann Butler, Kitty Byrd, Anne Camarda, Grace Carpenter, Katherine Cartwright, Susan Casey, Jessica Chandler, Terri Chiaverotti, Tom Cohen, Carol Collins, Nora Coronado, Terry Crain, Brenda Crist, Antoinette Crotty, JoAnn Davis, Pam Dedrick, Rome Doherty, Katie Donegan, Michelle Doyle, Camilla Edwards, Cath Eytcheson, Jeff Fairhall, Marlene Falkenbury, Danna Flood, Kathryn Foster, Shirley Fuller, Ion Gardescu, Barbara Garvick, Jay Gelzer, Diana L. George, Wendy Gerard, Helen Glazier, Irene Grebenschikoff, Chris Greenlee, Jim Griemes, Pamela Gross, Becca Hall, Holly Hamilton, Susan Harris, Anne Hay, Mary Helbach, Patricia Henry, Marni Hickey, Hart Hodges, Ellen Huss, Douglas G. Jackowich, Heidi James, Andy Jellin, Ann Johnson, Cynthia Johnson, Karen Johnson, Mary Johnston, Sheila Jones, Sylvia Jones, Tina Jones, Anne Kalliomaki, Nancy Kappelman, Googoo Kark, Janet Kimball, Ann Kosanovic-Brown, Kathy Krogslund, Sue Kwolek, Carol Landgraf, Nancy Langdon, Jill Larsen, Lise Larsen, Robin Laurich, John Leigh, Mary Ellen Lemen, Norman and Rosemary Lemoine, Pat Lewis, Carol Lindcroft, Jane Lister-Reis, Dana Loesche, Rich Macdonald, Mary Machala, Therese Maltzman, Christine Maxwell, Anne McClure, Lillian McElhoe, Dawn McGinnis, Tara McGown, Colleen McKinnon, Betsy McPhaden, Murray Meld, Gina Calder Messenger, Chris Moe, Elizabeth Moss, Joyce Moty, Jarvis Murphy, Kristen Myers, Claudia Carli-Nelson, Henrik Nordstrom, Julie North, Pamela Okano, Cassandra Olson, Rose Olson, Michael Ontko, Pat Nix, Carl Peterson, Rob Peterson, Patti Pitcher,

Laura Potash, Helen Powell, Carolyn Powley, Cheryl Purdie, Derrick
Rebello, Jennifer Reidel, Zarod Rominski, Cara Ross, Steven and Michele
Ross, George Rought, Sharron Ruhlen, Merrill Samuelson, Charlene
Schwartz, Gail Simon, Julie Smith, Helen Baker-St. John, Nancy Steffa,
Carol Stick, Betty Swift, Kirk Taylor, Marika Thompson, Cindy Tiehen,
Gail Tilmont, Pat Tomlin, Tim Towner, Terri Trimble, Passiko True,
Angie Walls, Wendy Weeks, Ana Wieman, Marty Wingate, Lois
Wornath, Margaret Wylie, Allison Young.

For information on community gardening, contact:

Seattle P-Patch Program
618 Second Avenue
Seattle, Washington 98104
phone (206) 684-0264

American Community Gardening Association
325 Walnut Street
Philadelphia, Pennsylvania 19106

INTRODUCTION

I tend to water my garden early in the morning, before the traffic picks up on 15th West. Most of the day some kind of breeze blows through the Interbay P-Patch, which lies in the trough between Magnolia and Queen Anne hills. But early in the morning, as the sun colors up the sky, the air is still, quiet. The first wedge of geese flies low over head, aiming north for the Ship Canal, following the water to wherever it is they are going. Smaller birds—sparrows and robins and the like—discuss this passage, or the rising of the sun, or the flavor of the worms. Who really knows what secrets birds share? They may even be talking about me, standing alone within the confines of an acre of growing food and flowers divided into 120 individual plots, squirting water from a leaking hose, the topsoil soaking it up like a brown blotter.

When winter had begun to loosen its grip but spring remained aloof, this ground was too waterlogged to work, to turn with spade or spading fork. Every gardener with a plot in the P-Patch had grown itchy in his or her own way. There were early lettuces to plant, beets, chard, spinach. Their places in the plot had been carefully considered all winter, the seeds ordered from catalogs well in advance. But digging in waterlogged ground does more damage than good, so this particular year began with the lesson of patience. The gardener is there to initiate, to encourage, to organize, to nurture, but never to call the shots. The rain would stop when it was good and ready.

Patience, like a well-planned conspiracy, has a certain payoff. For gardeners it is the connection between the food they grow and the food they put on the table. This Thanksgiving, for example, I will slyly add to the table a dish of cardoon stalks poached in a light tomato sauce. I will have used about 10,000 pounds of vine-ripened tomatoes to make the sauce, the benefits of my own crop. It will taste as far from a canned tomato sauce as one can get. And the cardoon—that cousin of artichoke with a flavor falling somewhere between delicate artichoke hearts and wild asparagus—well, it is only available to the cook who takes the trouble and has the patience to grow it. My Thanksgiving guests will nibble away at that dish and others, while conspiratorial murmurs of pleasure will circle the table.

But the gardener needn't wait for the traditional harvest banquet to enjoy the bounty of the garden. With the soil soaked deep enough to

satisfy the thirstiest of plants, I coil the hose for another gardener, then
return to my plot to fill a bowl with Puget Beauty strawberries and golden
raspberries. These two are the sweetest of their tribes. The strawberries
taste as though they have been individually injected with liqueur. The
first bite of golden raspberries makes all the nurturing worthwhile. Too
delicate for the commercial market, these berries are rarely found outside
the home garden. And when they are, they have usually been picked early,
on the hard side, so they can survive the ride to the store and the hours
they will languish before being purchased. I look into a bowl of treasure,
the sun catching on the droplets of water that cling to the berries, and I
plot the breakfast yet to come.

There is a rhythm in the garden, a drumbeat learned anew each year.
In the P-Patch, gardeners of many ages and differing backgrounds share
common ground. Whether they are passive or aggressive by nature, young
and energetic or old and aching, the garden demands of them a common
tuning. Bring to the garden what the gardener may, the plant will grow at
the pace it decides, and in the way it wishes. Gardening reveals a sense of

real time, the time it takes. In other words, there is nothing fast about the food the gardener grows.

So much care and planning has gone into the growing of the food that the preparation of it can't help but be just as careful and thoughtful. The time it takes to cook the meal, just as the time it has taken to grow the food, is the one ingredient in the bubbling pot of stew unique to each cook and gardener, a flavoring not available off the shelf in the neighborhood market. The recipes in this cookbook, all of them gleaned from the kitchens of Seattle's P-Patch gardeners, have this sense of time, this cycling of the seasons, in common.

The popular belief is that homegrown tomatoes picked fresh from the vine taste better than their store-bought counterparts because of some kind of immediacy. But this isn't the case. They taste better because a loving, caring gardener has puttered over the vines for their entire lives. Take that same care into the kitchen, add that kind of attention to the cooking at hand, and any of these recipes will have the flavorful impact of a vine-ripened, fresh-picked tomato.

Such are the secrets of the P-Patch, the sorts of things discussed by birds at the rising of the sun.

Schuyler Ingle
November 1993

MAP OF P-PATCH COMMUNITY GARDENS

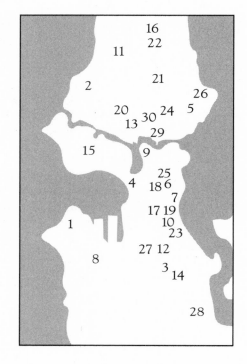

1. Admiral • 7 plots
   44th Avenue SW and SW Seattle Street
2. Ballard • 62 plots
   25th Avenue NW and NW 85th Street
3. Beacon • 18 plots
   2528 S Graham Street
4. Belltown • 40 plots
   Elliott Avenue and Vine Street
5. Burke Gilman Place • 25 plots
   Sandpoint Way NE and NE 52nd Street
6. Cherry Street • 10 plots
   29th Avenue and E Cherry Street
7. Colman Park • 47 plots
   32nd Avenue S and S Grand Street
8. Delridge • 32 plots
   *Delridge Way SW and
   SW Puget Boulevard*
9. Eastlake • 15 plots
   2900 Fairview Avenue E
10. Estelle Street • 16 plots
    S Estelle Street and Wetmore Place S
11. Evanston • 38 plots
    Evanston Avenue N and N 102nd Street
12. Ferdinand • 63 plots
    Columbia Drive S and S Ferdinand Street
13. Good Shepherd • 40 plots
    Bagley Avenue N and N 47th Street
14. Holly Park • 14 plots
    40th Avenue S and Webster Court
15. Interbay • 120 plots
    15th Avenue W and W Armour Street
16. Jackson Park • 35 plots
    10th Avenue NE and NE 133rd Street
17. Judkins • 21 plots
    24th Avenue S and S Norman Street
18. Marion • 15 plots
    24th Avenue E and E Marion Street
19. Mt. Baker • 29 plots
    29th Avenue S and S Grand Street
20. Phinney Ridge • 14 plots
    3rd Avenue NW and NW 60th Street

21. Picardo Farm • 281 plots
    26th Avenue NE and NE 82nd Street
22. Pinehurst • 15 plots
    12th Avenue NE and NE 115th Street
23. Rainier Vista • 13 plots
    4400 Tamarack Drive S
24. Ravenna • 11 plots
    5200 Ravenna Avenue NE
25. Republican • 13 plots
    20th Avenue E and E Republican Street
26. Sandpoint • 41 plots
    Sandpoint Way NE and NE 70th Street
27. Snoqualmie • 43 plots
    13th Avenue S and S Snoqualmie Street
28. Thistle • 110 plots
    *Martin Luther King Jr. Way and
    S Cloverdale Street*
29. University District • 55 plots
    8th Avenue NE and NE 40th Street
30. University Heights • 11 plots
    University Way NE and NE 50th Street

THE P-PATCH PROGRAM:
TWENTY YEARS OF
COMMUNITY GARDENING

*Cultivators of the earth are the most valuable of citizens. They are
the most vigorous, the most virtuous and they are tied to their country
and wedded to its liberty and interests by the most lasting bonds.*

— THOMAS JEFFERSON

Gardens are essential to the spirit and the soul. Local legend tells us that
in the 1920s the Picardo family's search for new farmland took them, by boat,
streetcar, and horse and buggy, to the area now known as the Wedgwood
district of Seattle. The 20 acres of farmland they bought extended from 25th
Avenue NE to 35th NE and from NE 82nd Street all the way to NE 75th.
The truck farm's produce was harvested daily for delivery to Pike Place
Market: truly fresh carrots, lettuce, celery, onions, spinach, and flowers. The
rich black soil was wonderfully productive. Imagine the greenhouses, barns,
orchards, workers' cabins, and bocci ball courts—it was a genuine Italian
working farm.

Over the years, parts of the farm were sold. People say that the black,
peaty soil of Dahl playfield was mined before the land was sold. Rainie
Picardo continued to farm his 2.5 acres well into the late 1960s. The early
1970s were years of change: Pike Place Market was dying; truck farming was
no longer profitable. The economic forecast for Seattle was cloudy, with a
chance of rain.

The 1970s were also years for grass roots dreams. Darlyn Rundberg Del
Boca, a University of Washington student, decided it was important for
children to learn how to grow food, and wanted to encourage them to grow
vegetables for Neighbors in Need, a precursor of today's food bank assistance
system. She was given permission to use part of the old Picardo family farm.
The children planted large plots of beans, broccoli, and cabbages. Parents
who helped were offered small spaces to "grow their own." The idea of community gardening sprouted alongside the vegetables. The concept wasn't
totally new, and it wasn't limited to Seattle. Community gardening was
resprouting across the nation from some very deep roots: village commons,
European allotment gardens, extended Asian family gardens, and wartime
victory gardens.

The early 1970s were years of building cooperative efforts. The newly
established Puget Consumers Co-op managed the Picardo farm site for a year.
The grass roots of the community garden extended to City Hall, and through

the efforts of City Councilman John Miller and Mayor Wes Uhlman (who had his own garden plot!), an ordinance was passed in 1974 authorizing a community garden program to promote recreation and open spaces. The program was adopted by the Department of Human Resources, and community gardens were offered throughout the city, united as the P-Patch Program. Officially, the "P" in P-Patch honored the Picardo family for making the initial land available. In addition, the letter stood for passionate people producing peas, pumpkins, potatoes, and peace in public. And like a phoenix, the program has risen to many challenges.

In keeping with the back-to-the-earth movement of the time, the P-Patch Program from the beginning allowed organic gardening only. Under the guidance of Edith Walden the gardens grew quickly to 10 sites in 1974. Work parties were held to make site improvements, including plumbing and water service. It was a relief not to have to carry water to Picardo Farm! With Glenda Cassutt as manager, the program grew to include 16 garden sites by the end of the decade. However, community gardens were still considered an "interim use" of land and some sites were built and then lost to "real" development. In the first 20 years of the P-Patch Program's history, 11 thriving gardens have met this fate.

In 1979 the fledgling P-Patch Advisory Council, a citizens group in support of community gardening, was incorporated, and not a moment too soon. The 1980s brought tight budgets, reduced services, and increased fees. Many garden plots were fallow, sites became overgrown, and community gardening almost died in Seattle. The efforts of the dedicated Advisory Council and program staff member, Brenda Baker, were impressive. True believers, undaunted, they persisted in restoring soil preparation and fertilizing services. Many gardeners who had found the early-season preparation too physically demanding joyfully returned to the gardens. The phoenix's flight path must have been over the P-Patches!

The early 1980s were not all hardship, however. The pairing of community development block grants and the skilled outreach of Barbara Heitsch, program coordinator, produced two large new garden sites for Southeast Asian refugee families who were then flooding into Seattle. Beginning in the mid-1980s, under the leadership of Nancy Allen and Barbara Donnette, P-Patches started sprouting in new Seattle neighborhoods. Capitol Hill regained a garden; Mt. Baker gardeners gained a new site; and Southeast Asian immigrants were able to find space at nearby expanded sites. Through the Gardenship Fund, generous gardeners helped their needy fellow gardeners pay plot fees. The Lettuce Link project began to coordinate delivery of more than 10 tons of donated produce to area food banks each year.

Finally the gardens were recognized for the unique opportunity they provided. In 1986 and 1987, four P-Patches were chosen as national community garden award winners. Winners exemplified cooperation, self-help, productivity, community involvement, and beautiful gardens. In 1987, the Pinehurst P-Patch, a national winner, won something even more important: the land was donated to the P-Patch Advisory Council, to be held in trust as the first truly permanent community garden. This step into permanence also marked a huge change in the perception of community gardens as a "real" development of land, no longer an interim use. It gave credibility to the gardens as vital, productive places, essential to urban well-being. In the same year, Seattle was honored to host the national conference for the American Community Gardening Association, at which Seattle's P-Patch Program was recognized as a national model for community gardening.

The 1990s arrived with unprecedented interest in community gardening and unforeseen opportunities for the P-Patch Program as a part of the new Department of Housing and Human Services. Even though the program has grown to include 30 sites and over 1,300 plots, there are still more than 600 households waiting to join. Neighborhoods are helping to build new garden sites with their sweat equity; community members are cultivating friendships as well as peas. They are helping those in need through food bank donations and teaching their children how food grows. The gardens provide peace as strong as any therapy can offer; they are expressions of love, trust, and vision. Thomas Jefferson was right.

Soups and Stews

The radio predicted cooler weather, and the wind was blowing up.
I bicycled up the hill right after dinner to my P-Patch, still bright
with the sunlight from the western sky that showed through
the black clouds swiftly rolling in. I covered the tomatoes with
plastic and tied up the raspberries that were in full bloom so the
wind wouldn't bend them over. The rest of the garden looked secure,
and I turned my bicycle homeward.

— An Evanston gardener

Sparkling Apple Soup with Kale

A TART APPLE AND HARD CIDER give spark to this winter soup, which calls for plenty of nutritious and abundant kale.

½ cup minced onions
1 clove garlic, minced
6 cups chopped kale
1 tart apple, peeled and chopped
2 tablespoons butter
3 tablespoons flour
5 cups Vegetable Broth (page 26)
1 cup hard apple cider
1 teaspoon minced fresh thyme
1 teaspoon minced fresh tarragon
freshly ground pepper to taste
1 cup milk
freshly grated nutmeg, for garnish

In a soup kettle, sauté the onions, garlic, kale, and apple in the butter until the onions are soft. Sprinkle in the flour and stir until brown. Add the broth, cider, thyme, tarragon, and pepper. Simmer for 30 minutes. In a food processor, puree the soup in batches; add the milk, reheat, and serve.
Serves 4.

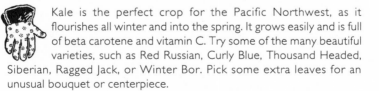

Kale is the perfect crop for the Pacific Northwest, as it flourishes all winter and into the spring. It grows easily and is full of beta carotene and vitamin C. Try some of the many beautiful varieties, such as Red Russian, Curly Blue, Thousand Headed, Siberian, Ragged Jack, or Winter Bor. Pick some extra leaves for an unusual bouquet or centerpiece.

THE CITY GARDENER'S COOKBOOK

Creamy Pumpkin Soup

SAVOR THIS SOUP in the fall, when the weather is crisp and the pumpkins are ripe. A pumpkin shell makes a charming soup tureen.

1 cup chopped onions
1 teaspoon butter
5 cups cubed pumpkin
2 cups Vegetable Broth (page 26)
1 cup milk
1 cup cream
¼ teaspoon freshly grated nutmeg
⅛ teaspoon cayenne pepper
fresh cilantro, for garnish

In a soup kettle, sauté the onions in the butter until translucent. Add the pumpkin and broth and cook until the pumpkin is soft. Puree in a food processor and return to the soup kettle. Add the milk and cream and heat thoroughly, but do not let the soup boil. Season with nutmeg and cayenne pepper. Garnish with cilantro. Serves 4 to 6.

 Early in the growing season, choose just the right baby pumpkin and lightly scratch a secret message on it with a pin. Scar tissue forms where you "wounded" the skin, and the message expands as the pumpkin grows. When the stem is dry and brittle, the pumpkin is ready to harvest. For longer storage, be sure to leave attached a stem at least 2 inches long.

Jack-o'-Lantern Soup

A JACK-O'-LANTERN *is too valuable to throw away after Halloween. The combination of the rich yellow pumpkin with red and green vegetables makes this soup especially appealing. A crusty black bread and cheese complete the meal.*

¼ cup chopped green peppers
½ cup chopped yellow onions
1 tablespoon olive oil
1 tablespoon flour
2 cups pumpkin puree
1 cup chopped tomatoes
2 cups Vegetable Broth
  (page 26)
¼ cup minced fresh parsley

¼ teaspoon minced fresh
  thyme
1 bay leaf
1 cup milk
salt to taste
freshly ground pepper to taste
curried pumpkin seeds,
  for garnish

To prepare the pumpkin puree, cut the jack-o'-lantern in half. Remove any candle wax and residual membrane or seeds. Invert the pumpkin cut side down on a baking sheet. Bake at 350° F until soft, about 30 minutes to 1 hour depending on the thickness of the pumpkin. Scoop out the meat and puree in a food processor for perfect pulp.

In a soup kettle, sauté the green peppers and onions in the oil until soft. Sprinkle in the flour and stir until lightly browned. Add the pumpkin puree, tomatoes, broth, parsley, thyme, and bay leaf. Cover and simmer for approximately 30 minutes, stirring occasionally. Remove the bay leaf and stir in the milk. Season with salt and pepper and heat thoroughly. Garnish with pumpkin seeds and serve. Serves 4 to 6.

To toast pumpkin seeds coat your hands with vegetable oil and rub the hulled seeds to grease them. Place the seeds on a cookie sheet, and bake at 375° F for 15 minutes. Season with salt and curry powder to taste. Bake another 5 minutes.

Beany Broccoli Soup

PUREED BEANS GIVE THIS SOUP *a lovely creamy texture without dairy products or added fat. Although white beans are called for in this recipe, many bush or pole beans have good-tasting seeds that you can use. Flageolets, small green or white kidney-shaped beans, work well because they cook down to a nice saucelike consistency. A dash of allspice lends a warm, aromatic touch.*

> 1 cup chopped onions
> 1 tablespoon olive oil
> 2 cups Vegetable Broth (page 26)
> 4 cups chopped broccoli florets
> 1 cup cooked white beans
> 1 bay leaf
> ¼ teaspoon ground allspice
> broccoli flower buds, for garnish

In a soup kettle, sauté the onions in the olive oil until tender. Add the broth, broccoli, beans, bay leaf, and allspice. Bring to a boil, reduce the heat, and simmer for about 20 minutes. Cool slightly, and remove the bay leaf. Puree the soup and serve hot, garnished with broccoli flower buds.
Serves 4.

All beans are relatively easy to grow, but it is very important not to work among your plants when the foliage is wet. The fungus botrytis develops in moist conditions and spreads easily by human hands. Weed and harvest before watering or after a streak of dry weather. The beans provide more nutrients after a sunny growing period.

Curried Broccoli Soup

WHEN THE WEATHER IS COLD and gray, enjoy this simple, sustaining soup. The flavor will inspire you to go out in the rain to harvest broccoli planted long ago in the days of summer.

1 tablespoon butter
¾ cup chopped onions
2 cloves garlic, chopped
¾ teaspoon curry powder
⅛ teaspoon freshly ground pepper
2 cups Vegetable Broth (page 26)
⅔ cup water
4 cups chopped broccoli
1½ cups cubed potatoes
1 cup milk

In a soup kettle, melt the butter and sauté the onions and garlic until tender. Add the curry powder, pepper, broth, and water and bring to a boil. Stir in the broccoli and potatoes. When the mixture returns to a boil, reduce the heat, cover, and simmer for about 20 minutes, or until the vegetables are tender. Puree the soup in batches in a food processor. Return the puree to the soup kettle, stir in the milk, and cook over low heat until hot.
Serves 6.

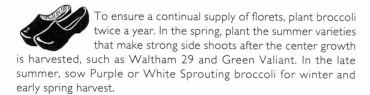

To ensure a continual supply of florets, plant broccoli twice a year. In the spring, plant the summer varieties that make strong side shoots after the center growth is harvested, such as Waltham 29 and Green Valiant. In the late summer, sow Purple or White Sprouting broccoli for winter and early spring harvest.

Cream of Greens Soup

FRESH, HAND-PICKED BROCCOLI, peas, and spinach, cool from the morning dew, are a rewarding medley of greens when seasoned with a light touch of nutmeg and blended with creamy yogurt and milk. You can substitute whatever greens are abundant in your garden.

½ cup chopped onions
1 cup chopped celery
6 cloves garlic, sliced
2 tablespoons butter
4 cups Vegetable Broth (page 26)
2 cups chopped broccoli
1 cup diced potatoes
¼ teaspoon salt
¼ teaspoon white pepper
¼ teaspoon freshly grated nutmeg
1 cup shelled fresh peas
1½ cups chopped spinach
1 cup milk
1 cup yogurt
1 grated carrot, for garnish

In a large soup kettle, sauté the onions, celery, and garlic in the butter. Add the broth, broccoli, potatoes, salt, pepper, and nutmeg. Simmer for 30 minutes, then add the peas and spinach and continue simmering for 10 minutes. In a food processor, puree the mixture and return to soup kettle. Add the milk and yogurt and heat thoroughly, but do not allow the soup to boil. Serve hot, topping each bowl with grated carrot.
Serves 6.

 In warm regions, New Zealand spinach is a perennial vegetable. Gardeners in colder regions like the maritime Northwest can still enjoy the vegetable, as it grows from spring seed into large succulent plants by midsummer. Harvest the largest leaves and those on the top 5 inches to ensure dense growth. A well-fertilized plant will continue producing until the first hard frost.

French Sorrel Soup

EARLY SUMMER IS THE TIME to make this tangy soup. New potatoes, Walla Walla sweet onions, and sorrel mature at the same time in the Northwest, so fill a garden basket. If you dried your hot red peppers from last season, add a few flakes as an accent.

> 3 cups chopped Walla Walla sweet onions
> 2 cups chopped sorrel
> 3 cups Vegetable Broth (page 26), divided
> 2 cups cubed and cooked new potatoes
> ¾ cup sour cream or yogurt
> ¼ cup milk
> dash red pepper flakes (optional)

In a saucepan, cook the onions and sorrel in half of the broth until the onions are tender. In a food processor, purée the mixture and return to the pan. Stir in the potatoes and remaining broth and heat thoroughly. Add the sour cream or yogurt and the milk. Heat gently to avoid curdling.
Serves 4.

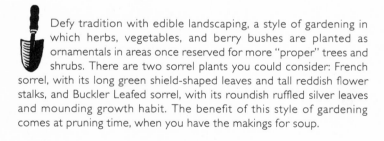

Defy tradition with edible landscaping, a style of gardening in which herbs, vegetables, and berry bushes are planted as ornamentals in areas once reserved for more "proper" trees and shrubs. There are two sorrel plants you could consider: French sorrel, with its long green shield-shaped leaves and tall reddish flower stalks, and Buckler Leafed sorrel, with its roundish ruffled silver leaves and mounding growth habit. The benefit of this style of gardening comes at pruning time, when you have the makings for soup.

Italian Greens Soup

THIS ITALIAN-STYLE RECIPE *calls for fava beans, greens, and toma-toes. Favas are large, starchy beans with an assertive flavor that is enhanced by the garlic, parsley, and basil. With lots of fresh chard, this soup makes a full meal. Serve it with a crusty Italian peasant bread.*

1 cup chopped onions
2 cloves garlic, minced
1 tablespoon butter
½ cup minced fresh parsley
2 tablespoons minced
   fresh basil
3 cups Vegetable Broth
   (page 26)
1 cup shelled fresh fava beans
4 cups chopped Swiss chard

1½ cups chopped tomatoes
1 teaspoon soy sauce or
   tamari
juice of half a lemon
¼ teaspoon freshly ground
   pepper
freshly grated Parmesan
   cheese, for garnish

In a large soup kettle, sauté the onions and garlic in the butter until soft. Then add the parsley and basil and continue cooking for 2 minutes. Pour in the broth, add the fava beans, and bring to a slow boil. Simmer for 20 minutes before adding the Swiss chard and tomatoes. Cook for an additional 15 minutes. Stir in the soy sauce or tamari, lemon juice, and pepper. Serve hot with Parmesan sprinkled on top.
Serves 6 to 8.

Swiss chard has big, glossy green leaves that hold up well over winter, even under a blanket of snow. It grows easily in the Pacific Northwest climate, provided you use a floating row cover to prevent leaf miner damage. Sow a short row anytime between April and July for almost a full year's harvest.

Leek, Potato, and Kale Soup

SERVE A PIPING HOT BATCH *of this wintertime soup on a blustery cold day. The long harvest-time, from fall into spring, of leeks, kale, and parsley makes them wonderful assets for the cooking gardener. Puree one of the cooked potatoes for a thicker consistency, or consider adding lentils, buckwheat, rice, or barley. The squeeze of lemon makes this stand above other ordinary leek and potato soups.*

3 cups thinly sliced leeks
3 cloves garlic, minced
3 tablespoons olive oil
3 cups cubed potatoes
5 cups coarsely chopped kale
1 cup chopped fresh parsley
1 tablespoon brown sugar
  or molasses

2 bay leaves
1 tablespoon Worcestershire
  sauce
8 cups Vegetable Broth
  (page 26)
juice of half a lemon
salt to taste
freshly ground pepper to taste

In a soup kettle, sauté the leeks and garlic in the oil until soft. Add the potatoes and continue cooking for 5 minutes, adding some of the broth if necessary to prevent sticking. Add the kale and parsley to the potato mixture and cook until tender, about 10 minutes. Stir in the bay leaves, brown sugar or molasses and the Worcestershire sauce. Add the broth and simmer for 30 minutes. Just before serving, stir in the lemon juice and season with salt and pepper. Serves 8 to 10.

Leeks grow well in the Northwest climate and soil. Several hardy varieties will survive wet winter weather. To blanch a large area on your leek plants, transplant the starts into a well-prepared, 5-inch-deep trench. Plant them deeply, right up to the first leaf axil. As the plants grow, hill up the soil, always staying just below the leaf axil. Keep the plants well fertilized and harvest before they flower.

Sweet and Sour Cabbage-Patch Soup

THERE'S NOTHING *quite as gratifying as harvesting vegetables for a wholesome soup. Fresh homemade tomato juice makes all the difference in this recipe.*

4 cups chopped Savoy cabbage
1 cup sliced carrots
½ cup chopped celery
3 bay leaves
3 cloves garlic, crushed
½ teaspoon freshly ground pepper
6 cups fresh tomato juice or puree
2 tablespoons honey
juice of 1 lemon
salt to taste

In a large soup kettle, place the cabbage, carrots, celery, bay leaves, garlic, and pepper. Pour the tomato juice or puree over the vegetables and bring to a boil. Reduce the heat and simmer for 30 minutes, until the vegetables are tender. Stir in the honey and lemon juice and simmer for 5 more minutes. Remove the bay leaves and salt to taste.
Serves 4.

Did you know that the fragrant, evergreen bay laurel tree grows majestically in the warm microclimates of the Pacific Northwest? Its leaves add a distinctive touch to soups, stews, and even ice cream. Only a few leaves are necessary to enhance a dish. The bay laurel is pretty enough to be a house plant, but if you can provide a warm spot, try growing it outdoors.

Smooth Vegetable-Peanut Soup

PEANUT BUTTER *gives vegetable soup richness and novelty, not to mention extra protein. This soup is blended to a creamy consistency and garnished with fresh herbs or ground peanuts.*

1 cup chopped onions
2 cloves garlic, chopped
1 tablespoon olive oil
¾ cup diced carrots
2 stalks celery, sliced
2 cups diced potatoes
1 cup chopped leeks, white part only
1 hot red pepper, seeded and finely chopped
4 cups Vegetable Broth (page 26)
⅓ cup peanut butter
salt to taste
freshly ground pepper to taste
minced fresh parsley, cilantro, scallions,
     or ground peanuts, for garnish

In a soup kettle, sauté the onions and garlic in the oil until the onions begin to soften. Add the carrots, celery, potatoes, leeks, hot pepper, and broth, then bring to a boil. Reduce heat and simmer, covered, until the vegetables are tender, about 10 minutes. Add some of the hot broth to the peanut butter to soften it, stir, and then return to the soup. Puree in a food processor and season with salt and pepper. Garnish and serve hot.
Serves 4.

Tomato-Ginger Soup

DELICATELY FLAVORED WITH GARLIC and ginger, this light tomato soup makes an elegant first course. Serve it garnished with lemon zest and yellow nasturtium blossoms. Don't wait for a special occasion; this soup is fine anytime.

5 cups seeded, coarsely chopped tomatoes

2 cloves garlic, minced

2 tablespoons butter

2 tablespoons grated fresh ginger

2 cups Vegetable Broth (page 26)

salt to taste

ground cinnamon or curry powder to taste (optional)

1 cup cooked rice

In a saucepan, sauté the tomatoes gently with the garlic and butter for a few minutes. Add the ginger, broth, salt, and optional seasonings. Cover pan and simmer for 20 minutes. In a food processor, puree the soup and return to saucepan. Add the rice, heat thoroughly, and serve.
Serves 4.

Growing good-tasting tomatoes in cool Pacific Northwest summers is a challenge. Be sure to choose an early variety that ripens 50 to 60 days from transplanting. Wait to plant until the night temperatures are above 50 degrees Fahrenheit, usually by mid-May. To encourage a strong root system, plant the transplants at a 45-degree angle, burying most of the stem under the ground. Provide early-season protection from temperature fluctuations with cloches made of plastic, floating row covers, or plastic milk jugs. Remove the cloches when the plants have outgrown them. Fertilize tomatoes during the summer, and keep water off the leaves to prevent diseases.

Freshest Pink Tomato Soup

WHEN FRESH TOMATOES are pureed, they assume a soft, foamy texture. By barely heating this puree with milk, you create not only the freshest but the lightest tomato soup you'll ever taste. Yellow tomatoes produce a marvelous cream-colored soup.

2 tablespoons butter
1 clove garlic, crushed
¼ cup thinly sliced red onions
2 tablespoons flour
2 cups milk
2½ cups peeled, seeded, and pureed tomatoes
1 teaspoon sugar
salt to taste
freshly ground pepper to taste
thinly sliced red onion, for garnish

In a saucepan, melt the butter. Add the garlic, onions, and flour and stir constantly over medium heat until brown and bubbly. Remove from heat and slowly stir in the milk until smooth. Gently scald the milk mixture over low heat. Add the tomatoes and sugar; heat gently to serving temperature. Season with salt and pepper. Serve immediately with red onion for garnish.
Serves 4.

 Longkeeper is an excellent variety of tomato to grow. These tomatoes are aptly named because they last all winter, provided you bring them in before cold weather. Like all tomatoes, they should be stored at room temperature rather than in the refrigerator. Orange on the outside and ruby red inside, Longkeepers make an attractive display in your kitchen. We've heard of one tomato that was kept into March; when sliced in two, the seeds had started to sprout. They were instantly planted and grew into perfect transplants for spring.

Tomato and Florence Fennel Soup

COMBINE TOMATOES AND FLORENCE *fennel from your garden (some-times called anise root) with white wine, bay leaves, and hot red pepper for a distinctive, slightly sweet, and elegant soup. Serve in white bowls garnished with a tender sprig of fresh fennel; the color scheme will please the most passionate food lover.*

4 cups peeled, seeded, and chopped tomatoes	1 bay leaf
1/2 cup chopped onions	1 teaspoon minced hot red peppers
3 cloves garlic, minced	1/8 teaspoon sugar
1 1/2 cups coarsely chopped Florence fennel bulb, divided	1 1/2 tablespoons anise liqueur (optional)
2 cups Vegetable Broth (page 26)	2 tablespoons minced fresh parsley
1/2 cup dry white wine	1 tablespoon butter
1/2 teaspoon salt	6 sprigs of fennel, for garnish

Cut the stems and leaves from the fennel bulb. Peel and discard any discolored outer sections of the bulb. Cut in half and wash under running water to remove all grit. Coarsely chop. In a soup kettle, combine the tomatoes, onions, garlic, 1 cup of the chopped fennel, broth, wine, salt, bay leaf, red peppers, and sugar. Bring to a boil and simmer over low heat for 15 to 20 minutes. Stir in the remaining 1/2 cup of fennel and continue cooking for 15 minutes. If using the liqueur, add now and simmer for 3 more minutes. Remove the soup from the heat, take out the bay leaf, and stir in the parsley and butter. Serve garnished with fennel sprigs.
Serves 6.

Florence fennel is grown mainly for the bulbous base, but the leaves and seeds can also be used. Harvest fennel when the bulb is 3 to 6 inches across, cut away the root and tops, and for the best flavor and texture, do not separate the stalks until ready to use. Because fennel stores best unwashed and will last for a maximum of 5 days in the refrigerator, harvest only as much as you need.

Radish and Champagne Soup

THE STRONG BITE of the peppery radish mellows in a luxurious base of Champagne and cream. The rosy pink color of this soup is truly beautiful.

    2 cups grated red radishes
    2 tablespoons olive oil
    4 cups fruity Champagne
      or sparkling wine
    3 tablespoons butter
    5 tablespoons flour
    1 cup chicken broth
    1 cup cream
    fresh chives, for garnish

In a soup kettle, sauté the radishes in the olive oil for about 5 minutes. Add the Champagne and simmer for 45 minutes. In a separate saucepan, melt the butter and sprinkle in the flour. Stir the flour constantly over medium heat until lightly browned. Add chicken broth slowly, stirring constantly until it reaches a gravylike consistency. Pour the thickened broth into the radish mixture and bring to a boil. Remove from the heat and slowly add the cream. Garnish with chives and serve.
Serves 6.

Red radishes can be planted as early as February under cloches. To prevent rust fly damage, protect them under a row cover until harvest. Water your crop evenly and deeply to keep the flavor mild and the flesh crispy.

Garden-Fresh Gazpacho

REWARD YOURSELF after a hot summertime gardening session with this cool, refreshing soup. Fresh tomato juice and chunks of ripe tomatoes are mixed with green pepper and cucumber for a bright-tasting seasonal favorite.

3 tomatoes, chopped	juice of half a lemon
1 medium onion, finely chopped	4 ice cubes
1 cucumber, chopped	salt to taste
½ green bell pepper, chopped	freshly ground pepper
1 clove garlic, minced	to taste
1 cup fresh tomato juice	cayenne pepper to taste

In a bowl, combine the tomatoes, onion, cucumber, green pepper, garlic, tomato juice, and lemon juice. Add the ice cubes and refrigerate for at least 2 hours. Season with the salt, pepper, and cayenne pepper, and serve chilled.
Serves 4.

 Because cucumbers come in many varieties, you should research the type of seeds or transplants to buy. Besides trailing or bush varieties, you'll want to know if you're planting a pickling or slicing cucumber. There are all-female (gynoecious) types, which produce only female flowers that result in fruit with fewer seeds. These can be grown under cover without the need for pollinators. There are Japanese, Middle Eastern, gherkin, lemon, and white cucumbers to choose from as well. For a successful cucumber crop, look for disease-resistant varieties, wait until the soil is warm, and provide plenty of compost and manure. Use black plastic mulch and a floating row cover to keep the soil warm, and water regularly. Harvest often so that the plants continue to produce fruit.

Green Thumb Gazpacho

RUSHING INTO THE KITCHEN with the bounty from your garden can cause panic when you realize that it won't fit in the refrigerator. This recipe condenses a large volume of greenery into a refreshing, mint-colored soup. Leeks, green peppers, cucumbers, arugula, and watercress are combined in minutes, but allow time for the soup to cool and the flavors to meld. You can substitute Chinese mustard greens or nasturtium leaves for the watercress.

2 cups chopped leeks	½ cup olive oil
1½ cups chopped green peppers	½ cup tarragon vinegar
4 cups peeled, seeded, and chopped cucumbers	1 teaspoon salt
4 cups minced arugula	½ teaspoon freshly ground pepper
2 cups minced watercress	pinch of cayenne pepper
1 large shallot, minced	dash of hot pepper sauce
3 cups yogurt	½ cup minced fresh dill

In a large bowl, combine the leeks, green peppers, cucumbers, arugula, watercress, and shallot. Whisk the yogurt, oil, vinegar, salt, pepper, cayenne, and hot pepper sauce together in a small bowl, add to the vegetables, and mix well. In a food processor blend the soup into a finely minced texture; do not puree. Stir in the dill and refrigerate for at least 4 hours before serving.
Serves 6.

Shallots are a mild-flavored member of the onion family. They require about 18 weeks from planting in February or March until harvest in July or August. One bulb, or set, will multiply into a cluster, so space them 6 inches apart. Although you can start them from seed, the sets are more forgiving in soil with low fertility or poor texture.

Chilled Zucchini-Curry Soup

GARDEN-FRESH ZUCCHINI, *cilantro, and parsley, wedded with Indian flavors, create a refreshing soup for a warm day. Curry powder can vary tremendously, but usually has for its three basic ingredients black pepper, coriander, and red chili. A complex blending of eleven additional spices gives each curry powder its unique flavor—experiment with different kinds.*

2 cups chopped zucchini
½ cup chopped red onions
½ cup chopped green peppers
1½ cups water
1 teaspoon curry powder
1 cup cream
1 cup yogurt
2 tablespoons soy sauce or tamari
1 tablespoon minced fresh cilantro
½ teaspoon ground turmeric
½ cup minced parsley

In a soup kettle, combine the zucchini, onions, peppers, water, and curry powder. Bring to a boil and cook until the vegetables are soft. Set aside to cool. In a food processor, puree the vegetable mixture, then stir in the cream, yogurt, soy sauce or tamari, cilantro, turmeric, and parsley. Serve cold.
Serves 4 to 6.

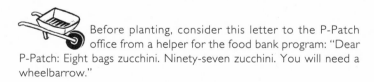 Before planting, consider this letter to the P-Patch office from a helper for the food bank program: "Dear P-Patch: Eight bags zucchini. Ninety-seven zucchini. You will need a wheelbarrow."

Garden Zucchini Soup

THIS IS A REFRESHING, *vibrant green soup so quick to make that it's almost like growing soup. It tastes great and will use those large zucchini that got away from you.*

6 cups sliced zucchini
1 onion, chopped
2 cloves garlic, minced
2 tablespoons olive oil
2 cups chicken broth
1 tablespoon curry powder
juice of half a lemon
salt to taste
chopped chives or green bell pepper, for garnish

In a soup kettle, sauté the zucchini, onion, and garlic in the olive oil for 10 minutes. In a food processor, puree the mixture. Return the puree to the soup kettle and add chicken broth, curry powder, lemon juice, and salt. Heat briefly and serve hot or cold. Garnish with chopped chives or green pepper.
Serves 6.

Zucchini need lots of room to grow. Some varieties trail like pumpkins, but the bush types are more common. Each plant spreads to a diameter of 4 feet, and the leaves themselves can grow to 18 inches across. Plant fast-growing spring crops like radishes or lettuces in the area that the zucchini will soon cover.

Chilled Vegetable and Buttermilk Soup

THREE ORDINARY GARDEN VEGETABLES *combine to form a light butter-milk soup, flecked with bits of red and green. The soup is prepared in advance and develops its fullest flavor as it chills. Enjoy it under the bright blue skies of summer with sprigs of fresh basil as garnish.*

2 tablespoons olive oil
1 large white onion, finely chopped
3 cups chopped zucchini
4 cups Vegetable Broth (page 26)
1 cup peeled, cored, and finely chopped tomatoes
1 cup buttermilk
¼ cup minced fresh basil
salt to taste
basil sprigs, for garnish

In a soup kettle, heat the oil and sauté until the onion is translucent. Add the zucchini and broth and bring to a boil. Cover, reduce heat, and simmer until the zucchini is tender, about 5 to 7 minutes. In a food processor, puree the mixture and pour into a large bowl. Add the tomatoes, buttermilk, basil, and salt. Cover and chill until cool, at least 2 hours. Stir thoroughly before serving. Garnish each serving with a basil sprig.
Serves 6 to 8.

Onions are plants tuned into the photo period of the season; in other words, they are sensitive to the length of day and night. The top will grow until the length of day triggers the bulb to develop. Fertilize early in the season: the size of the bulb is directly related to the size of the top growth. White onions, called for in this recipe, are as easy to grow from sets as the more common yellow ones.

Country Stew

IF YOU FIND that your snap beans have overripened, don't despair. Gather up the pods, dry the seeds, and save them for this hearty stew. The flavor of this vegetable medley intensifies overnight.

2 tablespoons olive oil	2 cups sliced carrots
1 cup chopped onions	2 cups peeled, cubed winter
1½ cups sliced leeks	squash or pumpkin
1 clove garlic, minced	2 cups peeled, cubed turnips
4 cups cooked white beans,	1 cup peeled, cubed kohlrabi
drained, liquid reserved	4 cups reserved cooking
½ cup minced fresh parsley	liquid or water
2 bay leaves	2 cups chopped Swiss chard
1 teaspoon minced fresh thyme	salt to taste
3 whole cloves	freshly ground pepper to taste

In a large soup kettle, heat the oil and add the onions, leeks, and garlic. Sauté until tender. Stir in the beans, parsley, bay leaves, thyme, cloves, carrots, squash or pumpkin, turnips, and kohlrabi. Pour in the liquid, cover, and cook over low heat. Slowly cook until the vegetables are tender, about 1 hour. Add the chard and simmer for another 20 minutes. Remove the bay leaves and season with salt and pepper.
Serves 8.

 It might take more planning and initial investment in seeds, but planting smaller quantities of several different types of vegetables allows for greater diversity in the garden as well as at the dinner table. Plant in succession for a longer harvest period, never leaving any soil vacant for long. If you buy the larger economy packages of seeds for your favorite vegetables, they can stay viable for 3 to 4 years in an air-tight container.

Fava Beans
with Roasted Red Peppers

FAVA BEANS, ALSO CALLED BROAD BEANS, *closely resemble limas but have longer pods and larger beans. Young favas can be cooked right in the pods, but mature ones must be shelled. This is a classic European way to prepare the assertively flavored favas: with olive oil, roasted red peppers, and wine.*

2 red bell peppers
2 cups shelled fresh fava beans
2 tablespoons olive oil
2 cloves garlic, finely minced
$\frac{1}{3}$ cup dry white wine
1 teaspoon minced fresh thyme

salt to taste
freshly ground pepper to taste
juice of half a lemon

Roast the red peppers over a gas flame or under a broiler, turning until all sides are uniformly charred. Remove from heat, and to help loosen the skins, place in a paper or plastic bag. When cool enough to handle, remove all the charred skin, rinse the peppers, and pat dry. Slice into thin strips, then cut the strips into 1- or 2-inch lengths. Set aside.

Blanch the fava beans for 30 seconds in boiling water. Drain and transfer to a bowl of cold water. Slip the beans out of their thick skins and place them in a bowl. Set aside. Heat the oil in a skillet and gently sauté the garlic until golden. Add the wine, thyme, and beans and simmer until tender, about 15 to 20 minutes, covered. Season with salt, pepper, and lemon juice.
Serves 4.

Bold, exotic fava bean plants improve your soil while they grow. Plant fava seeds in the fall to allow plenty of time for nitrogen-fixing bacteria to work for the winter-hardy plants. In spring, after the bean seeds are harvested, chop up the plants and dig them under for green "manure."

Heritage Bean and Pumpkin Stew

MANY GARDENERS ARE BECOMING *reacquainted with the colorful old bean varieties that are meant to be left on the vine to dry for fall and winter use. Jacob's Cattle, Vermont Cranberry, and Speckled Bay are a few varieties that do well in the Northwest. This warm and satisfying fall stew is a great way to enjoy your precious heritage beans. Follow tradition and save a few beans for next year's planting. Give yourself plenty of cooking time; the stew requires a slow baking process, which allows the flavors to commingle.*

1 cup dried beans,
 soaked overnight
1 large onion, sliced
1 clove garlic, minced
3 tablespoons minced
 fresh oregano
1 tablespoon chili powder
2 teaspoons olive oil

2 cups chopped tomatoes
3 cups Vegetable Broth
 (page 26)
1 green bell pepper, diced
1 ½ cups cubed pumpkin
1 cup fresh corn kernels

Drain the beans and set aside. In a skillet, sauté the onion, garlic, oregano, and chili powder in the oil for 5 minutes. Stir in the tomatoes and simmer for 5 minutes. Transfer the mixture to a 3-quart casserole. Add the drained soaked beans and broth. Bake 1½ hours at 375° F. Add the green pepper, pumpkin, and corn and bake an additional hour.
Serves 4.

An easy way to harvest bean seeds is to gather up the dry pods, put them in a pillowcase, and thrash them until the seeds have separated from the pods. In a rainy, cool area it is especially important to collect the pods before the fall rains come; wet pods must be shucked by hand. If they do get wet, find yourself a helper to make the time go by, and turn this task into a pleasant, old-fashioned way to catch up on conversation or songs unsung.

Winter Vegetable Stew

TAKE ADVANTAGE *of a sunny winter day to get outside and harvest your root crops. From your vegetable-laden pantry, gather some potatoes and winter squash and combine them with barley, freshly dug carrots, and turnips; toss in a bay leaf, and warm yourself with this hearty stew. This recipe gives you an excuse to pull from the freezer a few bags of peas that you shelled in the summer.*

2 tablespoons olive oil
2 cups chopped onions
    or leeks
2 cups diced potatoes
1½ cups diced carrots
1½ cups diced turnips
3 cups Vegetable Broth,
    divided (page 26)
1½ cups peeled, diced
    winter squash

1 bay leaf
2 teaspoons minced fresh
    winter savory
1 teaspoon minced fresh thyme
1½ cups cauliflower florets
2 cups peas
2 cups cooked barley
2 tablespoons freshly grated
    Parmesan cheese

In a skillet, sauté the onions or leeks in the oil until tender. Add the potatoes, carrots, and turnips, then stir in 1 cup of the broth. Continue cooking on low heat for 10 minutes. Add the squash, bay leaf, savory, and thyme and cook for 5 minutes. Stir in the cauliflower and remaining broth and cook for 10 minutes. Finally, add the peas and barley and cook for an additional 5 minutes. Remove from heat, let stand 10 minutes, and serve topped with Parmesan. Serves 8 to 10.

If your soil is not too wet to allow you an early start in late winter, plant the round-seeded varieties of peas as opposed to the "shrivelly" ones. Because of their shape, they are less likely to rot in February's cold soil. Look for peas that are resistant to diseases to ensure a successful crop. In maritime climates, peas will grow taller and take longer to mature than indicated on most seed packets.

Vegetable Broth

As WITH ANY RECIPE, *the final results will be only as good as the ingredients used. Start your broth with fresh vegetables that are at peak flavor. Cleaning out the refrigerator, as is often suggested for making stocks, is best done with the compost pile in mind. Any strong or off flavor will only intensify as the broth concentrates. Each batch can differ according to the intended soup or the season of harvest. Use any member of the onion family and root crops such as carrots and turnips, but avoid strongly flavored vegetables such as cabbage or asparagus. Potatoes will cloud the broth and are best used later to thicken the soup. Here is a suggested starting point. Vary it as you like and add your favorite herbs.*

4 cups chopped onions	2 bay leaves
2 cups chopped leeks, whites and greens	6 herb sprigs, such as oregano, thyme, or savory
3 cloves garlic, whole	1 teaspoon whole peppercorns
5 cups chopped carrots	4 quarts water
4 cups chopped celery, stalks and leaves	salt to taste

In a large kettle, combine the vegetables, herbs, peppercorns, and water. Bring to a boil and skim off any foam that forms. Reduce the heat and simmer for about 4 hours. Let cool slightly. Line a large bowl with several layers of cheesecloth and strain the mixture. Gather the pulp in the cloth, squeeze lightly, then discard. Rinse the kettle and return the liquid for further cooking. Reduce the stock to about 2 quarts by simmering another 1 to 1½ hours. Season with salt and cool as quickly as possible, uncovered, in the refrigerator. After it is cold, cover with a tight-fitting lid and use within 5 days. (Bacteria can grow in broth left at room temperature for too long, and a tightly covered warm broth in the refrigerator can sour or ferment.)
Makes 2 quarts.

Salads and Chilled Vegetables

Working a small patch of earth that has been worked year after year by loving hands renews my spirit. I feel the care the soil has received as I plant my seeds, and it gives me hope that people will learn to treat each other with the same kind of love that we bestow on our gardens.

— A Picardo farmer

Green Salad on the Wild Side

THE NEXT TIME you're in the garden mentally making up a green salad, let your imagination take over; there's more to life than lettuce. For greens, try young leaves of chard, kale, beets, orach, radicchio, endive, or your winter cover crop of corn salad. For flavor, try any herb such as basil, tarragon, parsley, arugula, nasturtium leaves, or cress. For color, it's fun to add flowers such as calendula petals, Johnny-jump-ups, chive blossoms, bean or Chinese snow pea flowers, borage blossoms, or rose petals. Red, white, or black currants; blueberries; blackberries; or red and white strawberries are a nice touch too.

Use the following sample recipe as a guide and feel free to substitute whatever is in your garden. Dress with Berry Vinaigrette (page 62).

1 head red butter lettuce, torn into bite-sized pieces
4 cups escarole or kale, torn into bite-sized pieces
1 cup chopped tender arugula
1 cup mixed baby greens
½ cup blackberries
¼ cup mixed flowers

In a large bowl, gently toss together the lettuce, escarole or kale, arugula, greens, berries, and flowers. Chill before serving. Sprinkle with Berry Vinaigrette or your favorite vinaigrette.
Serves 4 to 6.

Thinning your seedlings is a garden task that cannot be ignored. If not thinned, plants will compete for soil nutrients, robbing all the seedlings of their chance to grow well. One gardener says leaving plants too crowded is like putting them in prison. Use the tender young thinnings in salads.

Chicory Salad
with Curly Cress Dressing

THE NAMES ENDIVE AND CHICORY *are interchangeable. Both describe a large family of slightly bitter, lettuce-like greens. Some varieties are grown exclusively for blanching, such as Belgian endive or radicchio. The spreading, flattish heads of the frilly chicories or the more broad-leaved varieties, called escaroles, are grown and eaten just like lettuce. This salad features the tender, less bitter center of the chicory head.*

**2 heads of chicory, dark
outer leaves removed
1 head tender-leaf red lettuce**

CURLY CRESS DRESSING

**2 tablespoons fresh lemon
juice
2 tablespoons tarragon vinegar
1 tablespoon Dijon mustard
1 teaspoon minced
fresh tarragon**

**½ cup extra virgin olive oil
1 cup minced curly cress
leaves
salt to taste
freshly ground pepper
to taste**

Tear the chicory and lettuce into bite-sized pieces. Place in a large salad bowl and set aside. To make the dressing, combine the lemon juice, vinegar, mustard, and tarragon in a small bowl. Gradually whisk in the olive oil, followed by the cress leaves. Add salt and pepper and mix thoroughly. Slowly pour the dressing over the salad, using just enough to coat the leaves.
Serves 4 to 6.

There are four kinds of cress: garden or curly cress, winter or Belle Island cress, Upland cress, and watercress. All look somewhat like parsley and have a strong peppery, spicy flavor. Garden cress and Upland cress are annuals and grow easily in maritime Northwest gardens. Both mature in about 6 weeks, require moist soil, and are best used in the younger stages. Plant in spring or fall in rows 8 to 12 inches apart, and feed frequently with a high-nitrogen organic fertilizer.

Spinach and Strawberry Salad

OUR RECIPE TESTERS WERE HESITANT to try this shocking combination but were surprised at how much they enjoyed it. The subtle flavors of the spinach and fresh thyme are well balanced by the sweetness of the strawberries. For an elegant presentation, garnish this bold red and green salad with freshly harvested pea tendrils. Make the dressing in advance to allow the flavors to blend.

> **6 cups spinach leaves, torn into bite-sized pieces**
> **2 cups strawberries, washed, hulled and halved lengthwise**

DRESSING

2 tablespoons white wine vinegar	**¼ teaspoon salt**
½ teaspoon Dijon mustard	**freshly ground pepper**
2 teaspoons chopped fresh thyme	**to taste**
¼ cup minced red onions	**¼ cup olive oil**

On salad plates arrange the spinach and strawberries and keep chilled. To make the dressing, in a medium bowl, whisk together the vinegar, mustard, thyme, onions, salt, and pepper. Slowly add the olive oil, continuing to whisk, until the dressing is well combined. Drizzle the vinaigrette over each salad or toss all the ingredients in a salad bowl, combining well.
Serves 4.

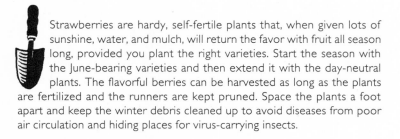

Strawberries are hardy, self-fertile plants that, when given lots of sunshine, water, and mulch, will return the favor with fruit all season long, provided you plant the right varieties. Start the season with the June-bearing varieties and then extend it with the day-neutral plants. The flavorful berries can be harvested as long as the plants are fertilized and the runners are kept pruned. Space the plants a foot apart and keep the winter debris cleaned up to avoid diseases from poor air circulation and hiding places for virus-carrying insects.

Mizuna Salad

THIS COMBINATION OF SNAP PEAS, *radishes, and the frilly leafed,
mild-flavored mustard green mizuna makes a piquant green salad that's
a little out of the ordinary. All of these vegetables are abundant in
June if planted in late March. (The optional mushrooms and jicama
must be purchased, as they do not grow in the Pacific Northwest.)*

    1 head butter lettuce, torn into bite-sized pieces
    4 cups chopped mizuna
    1 cup sliced snap peas
    2 green onions, sliced
    1 cup grated white radish or 1 cup sliced red radishes
    sliced mushrooms or grated jicama (optional)

DRESSING
    1 cup mayonnaise
    3 tablespoons soy sauce or tamari
    1 tablespoon seasoned rice vinegar
    toasted sesame seeds, for garnish

In a salad bowl, mix the lettuce, mizuna, peas, green onions,
and radishes. Add the optional vegetables and chill. To make the
dressing, combine in a small bowl the mayonnaise, soy sauce or
tamari, and rice vinegar. Thin with water, if necessary. Dress the
salad immediately before serving and garnish with the toasted
sesame seeds.
Serves 4 to 6.

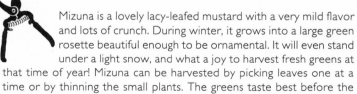

Mizuna is a lovely lacy-leafed mustard with a very mild flavor
and lots of crunch. During winter, it grows into a large green
rosette beautiful enough to be ornamental. It will even stand
under a light snow, and what a joy to harvest fresh greens at
that time of year! Mizuna can be harvested by picking leaves one at a
time or by thinning the small plants. The greens taste best before the
plant begins to flower.

Gingery Napa Salad
with Nasturtiums

THE DISTINCTIVE TANG *of orange and ginger stands out against the subtle flavor of napa, and the peppery nasturtium. A dash of hot sauce balances the dressing's sweetness.*

6 cups shredded napa cabbage

10 nasturtium leaves, sliced

1 cup julienned snow peas

1 cup grated carrots

1 tablespoon minced pickled ginger (optional)

toasted pine nuts and nasturtium flowers, for garnish

DRESSING

2 tablespoons toasted sesame oil

¼ cup seasoned rice vinegar

1 teaspoon grated fresh ginger

1 tablespoon grated orange zest

dash of hot pepper sauce

salt to taste

In a salad bowl, combine the cabbage, nasturtium leaves, snow peas, carrots, and pickled ginger, if used. Chill the salad. To make the dressing, whisk together the oil, vinegar, ginger, orange zest, hot sauce, and salt. Allow the flavors to meld while the salad chills. When ready to serve, dress the salad, and garnish with pine nuts and nasturtium flowers.
Serves 6.

 Plant napa cabbage in rich, well-worked soil, add lots of lime and well-rotted manure, and keep it growing steadily. Since temperatures fluctuate more in early spring, sow the seeds in midsummer or plant transplants outside in August for a greater chance of success. Watch for slugs; they find new transplants delicious.

Arugula and Beet Salad

ARUGULA, ALSO KNOWN AS ROQUETTE *or rocket cress, has a smoky, nutty flavor when young and a peppery, mustardy flavor when the plant matures. Originally from Italy, arugula grows well in the Pacific Northwest. At any stage of growth, its leaves contrast in taste and texture with the earthy beetroot flavor. The flowers, which have a honey-roasted flavor, make a lovely garnish for salads.*

8 medium beets
6 tablespoons olive oil
2 tablespoons wine vinegar
2 tablespoons minced fresh chives
salt to taste
freshly ground pepper to taste
¾ cup coarsely chopped arugula
1 hard-boiled egg, finely chopped (optional)

In a covered baking dish, bake the beets at 350° F until tender, about 1 hour. Cool, then peel and slice the beets. Set aside in a medium bowl. To make the dressing, combine the oil, vinegar, chives, salt, and pepper in a small bowl and pour over the beets. Marinate for 30 minutes. Gently toss in the arugula and egg, if used. Serve immediately.
Serves 4 to 6.

 Arugula thrives in the spring and fall. Sow the seed as soon as the ground is workable and make successive sowings. In its later, hotter stage, arugula is a fine substitute for watercress in soups, salads, and sandwiches. One plant, allowed to set seed, will produce an abundance of plants for the seasons ahead.

Beet Salad

THERE IS NOTHING *more satisfying to a gardener than to convert a beet hater. Serve your guests a scoop of this bright magenta salad in a cup of bibb lettuce. Add a sprig of fresh dill or fennel on the side, sit back, and enjoy their delighted reaction.*

6 medium beets, cooked, peeled, and diced
2 green onions, chopped
2 tablespoons mayonnaise
2 teaspoons fresh lemon juice
freshly ground pepper to taste
2 tablespoons minced fresh dill

In a bowl, mix the beets and green onions with the mayonnaise. Add the lemon juice, pepper, and dill and toss gently. Serve warm or cold.
Serves 4.

 Beets are a great "double-duty" crop because both the tops and bottoms are edible. Easy to grow in the Pacific Northwest, all they need is a little lime and some manure added to the soil before sowing. Just remember to keep the soil evenly moist, otherwise tough ring zones will form during a drought. Try all colors: the sweet, white, nonstaining fall beet; the glowing golden beet; the mild pink beet; and the more common red beet, which comes in round and cylindrical shapes.

Broccoli Salad
with Lemon-Yogurt Dressing

FRESHLY SQUEEZED LEMON and cool yogurt are featured in this refreshing salad. Homegrown tomatoes, fresh off the vine, provide a mellow flavor and yielding texture in contrast to the crisp broccoli and tart dressing.

6 cups chopped broccoli
1½ cups chopped tomatoes

LEMON-YOGURT DRESSING
3 green onions, minced
juice of 1 lemon
½ cup yogurt
¼ teaspoon salt
2 teaspoons chopped fresh tarragon
2 teaspoons chopped fresh basil
freshly ground pepper to taste

Lightly steam the broccoli until just tender, about 5 minutes. Rinse under cold water, drain, and place in a serving bowl. Add the tomatoes to the broccoli. To make the dressing, combine the green onions, lemon juice, yogurt, salt, tarragon, basil, and pepper. Pour over the vegetables and toss gently until well mixed. Chill for at least 1 hour before serving.
Serves 4.

Many plants are called broccoli, including Calabrese, Romanesco, Purple or White Sprouting, and broccoli de rabe. Seed sources of yesteryear refer to winter cauliflower as broccoli, listing white and red varieties. Romanesco has been thought of as a pale green cauliflower hybrid, and broccoli de rabe, whose flower buds are picked in early spring like broccoli, is really a turnip. As a general term, "broccoli" refers to a plant that sprouts side shoots once the head is cut. Cauliflower, on the other hand, is only harvested once.

Carrot-Tomatillo Salad

TRY THIS COMBINATION in the fall, when tomatillos are ripening fast and your second crop of cilantro is in full glory. It is a nice change from raisin-carrot salad and goes well with Mexican-style food and fish. If you don't have tomatillos, try grated apples. You can also use ground cherries, a yellow-orange novelty fruit closely related to tomatillos.

5 cups coarsely grated carrots
2 tablespoons chopped fresh cilantro
2 to 3 tomatillos ripened to the light green stage,
　husked and chopped
2 tablespoons apple juice concentrate

In a large bowl, combine the carrots, cilantro, and tomatillos. Moisten with the apple juice concentrate. Serve chilled. Serves 6 to 8.

For this recipe, the tomatillos should be ripened to the light green stage, when they are at their sweetest. (Tomatillos in the earlier, dark green stage are better for salsas.) Grow the variety Indian Strain that is claimed to be sweeter than the common salsa tomatillo. Try growing ground cherries, also called cape gooseberries or husk cherries. Start cherries outdoors from seed in late spring and thin so that each plant has a square foot to grow. The fruit ripens best after falling from the plant, hence the name. Even though the "cherries" come in their own wrapper, late-season mulching of black plastic or cloth will help keep them cleaner.

Cauliflower and Apple Salad

DID YOU KNOW *that there are purple varieties of cauliflower? Try growing Violet Queen or Purple Cape. This salad can be made with purple or white cauliflower or a combination of both. Crisp fall apples lend a sweetness that will please even young children.*

4 cups cauliflower florets, thinly sliced
3 red apples, diced
1 cup sliced celery
3 small green onions, sliced
½ cup chopped fresh parsley
¼ cup red wine vinegar or fruit vinegar
¼ cup walnut oil
½ cup cashews (optional)

In a large bowl, combine the cauliflower, apple, celery, onions, and parsley. Refrigerate until crisp. In a small bowl, combine the vinegar and oil. Mix well. Pour over the salad and toss lightly. Add cashews just before serving, if desired.
Serves 6.

To keep cauliflower heads blanched and clean, bend in the central leaves or tie them together (there are self-blanching varieties whose central leaves grow inward). Be sure to peek in often to observe when it is time to harvest. The cauliflower heads, sometimes called curd, should be on the small, tight side rather than loose and beginning to flower. Purple cauliflower needs sun to develop full color, so leave it exposed.

Cool Mint and Cucumber Salad

GARDENERS CAN TAKE ADVANTAGE *of a wide range of plant varieties. There are 20 species and more than 2,300 different varieties of mint. Try some of the more unusual ones, such as lemon balm, black peppermint, or apple mint. This refreshing salad with its creamy dressing looks beautiful nestled into a soft green bed of butter lettuce. It can be assembled on a large platter or served on individual plates.*

5 cups coarsely chopped cucumbers
½ teaspoon salt
2 cups yogurt
3 cloves garlic, minced
2 tablespoons fresh lemon juice
1 tablespoon minced fresh dill
2 tablespoons extra virgin olive oil
2 tablespoons minced fresh mint
10 large butter lettuce leaves, rinsed and chilled
salt to taste
freshly ground pepper to taste

In a colander, sprinkle the cucumbers with the ½ teaspoon salt, toss to coat and set aside to drain for 15 minutes. Place the cucumbers in a large bowl and add the yogurt, garlic, lemon juice, and dill. Toss gently, cover, and chill at least 3 hours. Add the olive oil and half of the mint leaves. Serve on a bed of lettuce sprinkled with the remaining mint, salt, and pepper.
Serves 4 to 6.

 Most mints propagate by rapidly spreading underground runners. If allowed to flower, they can also reseed, but the flavor is best before the mint blooms. Keeping mint contained is one of the biggest challenges to gardeners. Harvest and enjoy as much as you can and share with friends. Plant the varieties that you enjoy eating, as they are less likely to outgrow you.

Fresh Soybean and
Cranberry Bean Salad

THIS IS A TRUE GARDENER'S SALAD *because shell beans, with mature,
still-moist seeds within the bean pod, are available only to home gardeners. Don't be misled by the word cranberry—it refers not to the taste
but to the beautiful, speckled red markings on both the white pods and
the beans themselves. Here's a delightful opportunity to unveil a more
unusual bean salad, enlivened with ever-abundant, garden-fresh mint.*

1 cup shelled fresh cranberry beans
1 cup shelled fresh soybeans
2 tablespoons minced fresh mint
2 tablespoons fresh lime juice
1 clove garlic, minced
tomato slices, for garnish

In a saucepan, cover the cranberry beans and soybeans with water.
Bring to a boil and cook 5 to 10 minutes, until tender. Drain and
put in a salad bowl. Add mint, lime juice, and garlic and toss gently.
Chill to allow flavors to commingle. Garnish with tomato slices.
Serves 4.

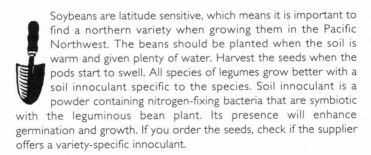

Soybeans are latitude sensitive, which means it is important to
find a northern variety when growing them in the Pacific
Northwest. The beans should be planted when the soil is
warm and given plenty of water. Harvest the seeds when the
pods start to swell. All species of legumes grow better with a
soil innoculant specific to the species. Soil innoculant is a
powder containing nitrogen-fixing bacteria that are symbiotic
with the leguminous bean plant. Its presence will enhance
germination and growth. If you order the seeds, check if the supplier
offers a variety-specific innoculant.

Dilled Carrot and Pea Pod Salad

PEAS AND CARROTS *are classic partners; sugar snaps have made the combination even better. Celebrate spring by gathering your first early crop of peas and carrot thinnings.*

3 cups whole baby carrots, trimmed
3 cups snow peas or sugar pod peas, trimmed

DRESSING
¼ cup fresh lemon juice
¼ cup minced fresh dill
2 tablespoons extra virgin olive oil
½ teaspoon salt
freshly ground pepper to taste

Steam the carrots and peas until just tender, about 3 to 5 minutes. To make the dressing, in a small bowl mix the lemon juice, dill, oil, salt, and pepper. Pour over the carrots and peas and toss to coat evenly. Refrigerate 6 hours or up to 2 days.
Serves 6 to 8.

Snap peas arrived on the gardening scene quite recently and have since become popular. They have the highest crop yield of any pea and grow sweeter as they enlarge. Sugar snaps and most other snap varieties are not resistant to pea enation virus, which causes the plants to yellow and die from the ground up. To avoid this problem, plant very early (mid-February, weather permitting) or try growing Sugar Daddy, a newer introduction that is more resistant to disease.

Fresh Parsnip Salad

PARSNIPS ARE THE QUIET *relative of the more popular and well-known carrot. Their sweet, nutty flavor is best in the winter after a freeze. Tangy and multicolored, this grated root salad offers a surprising blend of earthy and sweet flavors. From skeptics not enthusiastic about trying raw parsnips expect rave reviews.*

> 2 cups grated parsnips
> ½ cup chopped green bell peppers
> 1 cup grated carrots
> 1 medium apple, peeled and grated

DRESSING
> ¼ cup sour cream or yogurt
> 2 tablespoons peanut oil
> 2 tablespoons cider vinegar
> 1 teaspoon soy sauce or tamari
> ½-inch piece fresh ginger, peeled

In a medium bowl, combine the parsnips, peppers, carrots, and apple and set aside. In a small bowl, mix together the sour cream or yogurt, oil, vinegar, and soy sauce or tamari. Squeeze the ginger through a garlic press. Add the juice only to the sour cream mixture and discard the pulp. Pour the dressing over the salad and toss gently.
Serves 4.

Parsnip roots develop to a length of 12 to 18 inches and become distorted in a heavy or rocky soil. To grow good-sized parsnips even in hard clay soils, "rock bar" a cone-shaped hole about 2 feet deep in the center. Backfill this hole with a soft, rich soil. Sow a few seeds and later thin to one plant per cone. Space cones 8 to 10 inches apart. With even watering you should end up with a prize winner to take to the county fair.

Green and Yellow Squash Salad

THE EXTRAVAGANT BOUNTY *of squash plants allows for traditional uses as well as lots of experimenting with the fruit at all ages and stages. Delicate young, dark green zucchini and bright yellow crookneck squash are a pleasing combination. Capture the flavor of sun-soaked squash in this simple, delicately herbed salad. Raw or lightly steamed, this salad might become one of your favorite recipes for summer squash.*

> **4 cups julienned zucchini**
> **4 cups julienned yellow crookneck squash**

DRESSING
> **½ cup sliced red onions**
> **¼ cup fresh lemon juice**
> **¼ cup minced fresh parsley**
> **2 tablespoons minced fresh basil leaves**
> **1 tablespoon minced fresh oregano**
> **3 tablespoons olive oil**
> **freshly ground pepper to taste**

In a large saucepan, lightly steam the zucchini and crookneck squash until barely tender but still crunchy. Combine the onions, lemon juice, parsley, basil, oregano, and olive oil in a small bowl. Pour the dressing over the salad and toss gently. Season with freshly ground pepper. Chill before serving.
Serves 6 to 8.

Italian Zucchini Salad

A BASIC RECIPE for the prolific zucchini, this salad tastes just as good the next day. For a crunchy variation, add the zucchini raw instead of steaming it.

4 cups sliced zucchini
1 medium onion, thinly sliced
2 cloves garlic, minced
1 cup sliced mushrooms
1½ cups chopped tomatoes

DRESSING
¼ cup olive oil
3 tablespoons wine vinegar
1 teaspoon salt
⅛ teaspoon freshly ground pepper
2 tablespoons chopped fresh oregano

In a small saucepan, steam the zucchini until just barely tender. Refresh in cold water, drain and place in a large bowl. Add the onion, garlic, mushrooms, and tomatoes and set aside. To make the dressing, combine in a small bowl the oil, vinegar, salt, pepper, and oregano. Pour the dressing over the vegetables and toss gently. Refrigerate for several hours.
Serves 6 to 8.

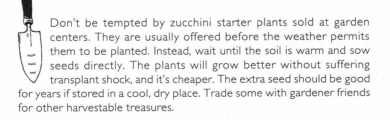

Don't be tempted by zucchini starter plants sold at garden centers. They are usually offered before the weather permits them to be planted. Instead, wait until the soil is warm and sow seeds directly. The plants will grow better without suffering transplant shock, and it's cheaper. The extra seed should be good for years if stored in a cool, dry place. Trade some with gardener friends for other harvestable treasures.

Tangy Eggplant Salad
with Nasturtium Capers

THE ELEGANT PEAR-SHAPED EGGPLANT, *with its glossy purple skin, is an ornamental as well as edible vegetable. Its "meaty" texture rewards those who create this hearty salad packed with garden-fresh tomatoes and herbs. Capers, called for in this recipe, are the expensive pickled buds of a Mediterranean bush. You can substitute your own pickled, easy-to-grow nasturtium buds. But if you plan to harvest the nasturtium flower buds, remember to grow a few extra plants, so that you can still enjoy the colorful flowers. The green seeds of the nasturtium can also be used, but the flavor is stronger.*

6 cups peeled, cubed eggplant

¼ teaspoon salt

juice of half a lemon

½ cup finely chopped celery

½ cup chopped onions

2 cups chopped tomatoes

8 to 10 large lettuce leaves

sliced stuffed green olives, as garnish (optional)

DRESSING

2 tablespoons red wine vinegar

1 tablespoon minced fresh oregano

1 tablespoon minced fresh chives

1 tablespoon minced fresh parsley

1 clove garlic, minced

1 tablespoon nasturtium capers
(recipe follows) or imported capers

In a medium saucepan, cook the eggplant cubes in boiling water to cover, salt, and lemon juice until soft, about 5 minutes. Drain well and place in a large bowl. Add the celery, onions, and tomatoes to the eggplant and mix thoroughly. To make the dressing, combine the vinegar, oregano, chives, parsley, garlic, and capers. Pour over the vegetables and gently toss. Arrange the salad on lettuce leaves and garnish, if desired, with the olive slices. Serves 6 to 8.

NASTURTIUM CAPERS

3 cups green nasturtium flower buds or seeds
½ cup salt
1 quart water
distilled vinegar, enough to cover buds
sterilized jars

Wash the nasturtium buds and place in a bowl. Mix the salt and water to make a soaking brine. Cover the buds with the brine and, if necessary, weight them to keep them submerged. Soak for 24 hours. Remove the buds from the brine and soak in cold water for about 1 hour. Drain and pack the buds in sterilized jars to within ½ inch of the top. Bring the vinegar to a boil and pour into the jars. If you are planning to eat the capers within a few weeks, simply refrigerate; otherwise, seal and process in a boiling water bath for 15 minutes.

Purple and Gold Slaw

STRIKINGLY BEAUTIFUL, *yet simple to make, this salad is subtly complex.*

4 cups shredded red cabbage
½ cup thinly sliced red onions
2 golden apples, diced
⅓ cup golden raisins

DRESSING
½ cup mayonnaise
¼ cup sweetened rice vinegar
⅛ teaspoon mace

In a large bowl, combine the cabbage, onions, apples, and raisins. To make the dressing, mix the mayonnaise, vinegar, and mace together. Pour over the other ingredients and toss gently. Serve chilled.
Serves 4 to 6.

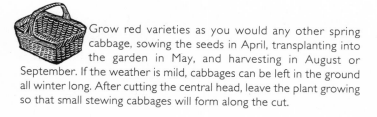 Grow red varieties as you would any other spring cabbage, sowing the seeds in April, transplanting into the garden in May, and harvesting in August or September. If the weather is mild, cabbages can be left in the ground all winter long. After cutting the central head, leave the plant growing so that small stewing cabbages will form along the cut.

Sweet Pepper Slaw

TRADITIONAL COLESLAW brings to mind a rich, high-fat salad. Instead of mayonnaise, this salad uses distinctively light rice vinegar, which lowers the fat content and lets the colorful red and green peppers shine through.

7 cups shredded green cabbage
1 large green bell pepper, coarsely chopped
1 large red bell pepper, coarsely chopped
1 cup sliced celery
3 green onions, chopped
2 tablespoons peanut oil
2 tablespoons seasoned rice vinegar
1 tablespoon of either poppy seeds, dill seeds, celery seeds, minced cilantro, parsley, or fennel

In a large bowl, combine the cabbage, green and red peppers, celery, and green onions. Mix the oil and vinegar and pour over the vegetables. Sprinkle with the tablespoon of seasoning. Combine thoroughly, cover, and chill several hours before serving. Serves 8 to 10.

 Growing peppers in the Northwest is a bit of a challenge. Pick an early variety and do all you can to keep them hot and well watered. You can try growing red, green, white, yellow, lavender, orange, chocolate-brown, or purple varieties. A novice gardener we know planted a new variety, Chocolate, and a standard hot pepper in the hope that they would cross and he'd have hot chocolate peppers.

Marinated Vegetables

WHETHER SERVED AT PARTIES, *as an antipasto side dish, or simply right out of the refrigerator, these won't last long. The explosion of color is as dazzling to your eye as the taste is to your palate.*

2 cups trimmed green beans
3 cups broccoli florets
2 cups cauliflower florets
4 carrots, diagonally sliced ¼ inch thick
10 large mushrooms, halved
1 red bell pepper, cut into thin strips

MARINADE
½ cup olive oil
¼ cup red wine vinegar
2 large cloves garlic, pressed
1 teaspoon honey
½ teaspoon salt
1 teaspoon dry mustard
2 tablespoons minced fresh basil
½ teaspoon freshly ground pepper
⅛ teaspoon freshly grated nutmeg

Quickly steam the green beans, broccoli, cauliflower, and carrots until only slightly tender, about 3 to 5 minutes. Refresh under cold water, drain, and place in a large bowl. Add the mushrooms and red pepper and set aside. Prepare the marinade by whisking together the olive oil, vinegar, garlic, honey, salt, mustard, basil, pepper, and nutmeg. Pour over the vegetables and toss gently. Refrigerate 6 hours or overnight, turning occasionally to coat.
Serves 6 to 8.

Parsley-Packed Peppers

THIS IS A QUICK and easy summer salad that can be made up to 5 hours in advance. If desired, the peppers may be roasted first to add a smoky flavor and softer texture. The filling is also wonderful stuffed into cored tomatoes. Save the tomato pulp for soup or sauce, or try growing the latest, a "stuffing" tomato. If you have tofu-phobia, try cottage cheese instead.

½ pound firm tofu
½ cup finely chopped mushrooms
½ cup chopped cucumber
½ cup chopped fresh parsley
½ cup chopped watercress or mustard greens
2 teaspoons soy sauce or tamari
2 tablespoons nutritional yeast (optional)
2 tablespoons chopped fresh dill
2 medium green bell peppers
4 slices cucumber, for garnish

Rinse the tofu and crush it in a medium bowl. Mix in the mushrooms, cucumber, parsley, and watercress or mustard greens. Stir in the soy sauce or tamari, yeast, if used, and dill. Cut the peppers in half lengthwise, core, and deseed. Stuff each half with the tofu mixture. Garnish with a cucumber slice.
Serves 4.

The stuffing tomato is a novel variety that grows in the shape of a pepper and remains hollow in the middle. A yellow one is also available. Although the days to maturity listed in some catalogs are not guaranteed, a tomato or pepper said to mature in 76 days or less should ripen in a cooler region. Bell peppers bred for northern areas or for patio growing ripen more reliably than the large Whopper or California Wonder types.

Brussels Sprouts
with Walnut Vinaigrette

GARDEN-FRESH BRUSSELS SPROUTS *are an entirely different vegetable from those mushy, bitter little balls we were forced to eat as children. Newly harvested sprouts just touched by frost are sweet, crisp, and almost buttery. You can add Italian herbs such as oregano, marjoram, or thyme to the vinaigrette before chilling overnight.*

> **4 cups Brussels sprouts, trimmed**
> **4 tablespoons wine vinegar**
> **3 tablespoons honey**
> **1 tablespoon Dijon mustard**
> **½ cup walnut oil**
> **salt to taste**
> **freshly ground pepper to taste**
> **1 cup walnuts, coarsely chopped**

To help the Brussels sprouts cook evenly, cut an "X" in the base of each. In a saucepan, steam the sprouts until just tender, about 5 to 7 minutes. In a large bowl, whisk together the vinegar, honey, mustard, oil, salt, and pepper. Toss the hot Brussels sprouts and walnuts in the dressing and refrigerate overnight.
Serves 4 to 6.

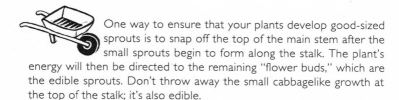

One way to ensure that your plants develop good-sized sprouts is to snap off the top of the main stem after the small sprouts begin to form along the stalk. The plant's energy will then be directed to the remaining "flower buds," which are the edible sprouts. Don't throw away the small cabbagelike growth at the top of the stalk; it's also edible.

Asian Noodle Salad

SPRINGY WHITE NOODLES, *crunchy red and green vegetables, and a light dressing are combined in a refreshing salad that's easy to eat by the bowlful. The rice noodles and fish sauce can be found in the Asian food section of most grocery stores.*

1 package rice noodles (3 to 4 ounces)
½ cup chopped green onions
6 radishes, sliced
1 cucumber, quartered and diced
2 cloves garlic, minced
¾ cup peeled, cooked shrimp (optional)
toasted sesame seeds, for garnish

DRESSING
¼ cup toasted sesame oil
2 tablespoons seasoned rice vinegar
2 teaspoons fish sauce
¼ teaspoon salt
½ teaspoon minced fresh fennel leaves
½ teaspoon minced fresh marjoram
½ teaspoon minced fresh oregano

Break the rice noodles in half and cook in boiling water for 1 to 2 minutes until soft. Drain, rinse in cold water, drain again, and place in a bowl to cool. Add the green onions, radishes, cucumbers, garlic, and shrimp, if used. Set aside. To make the dressing, place the sesame oil, vinegar, fish sauce, salt, fennel, marjoram, and oregano in a small bowl. Mix thoroughly and pour over the salad. Garnish with the sesame seeds. Refrigerate for 1 or 2 hours before serving.
Serves 4.

Chinese Rice Salad with Snow Peas

GRAINS SUCH AS RICE *are an excellent source of low-fat protein. Usually thought of as a hot item, rice exhibits its versatility in this salad by becoming the perfect base for concentrating the flavors of the marinade. An assortment of garden-fresh vegetables completes the interplay of flavors.*

> 2 cups snow peas, sliced lengthwise
> 1 cup chopped broccoli
> 1 cup cherry tomatoes, halved
> 1 cup diced yellow bell peppers
> ¾ cup diced red onions
> 4 cups cooked rice

DRESSING
> ¼ cup soy sauce or tamari
> ½ cup minced fresh parsley
> 2½ tablespoons Chinese black vinegar or 1½ teaspoons
>   Worcestershire sauce
> 1 teaspoon sugar
> 1 teaspoon toasted sesame oil

Steam the snow peas and broccoli together until barely tender, about 3 to 5 minutes. Refresh under cold water, drain, and place in a large serving bowl. Add the cherry tomatoes, yellow pepper, onions, and rice and toss gently. To make the dressing, whisk together the soy sauce or tamari, parsley, black vinegar or Worcestershire sauce, sugar, and oil. Pour over the vegetables and stir. Serve at room temperature.
Serves 6.

Sow the flat snow or Chinese peas, as early as you can, and harvest them when small and tender. Many snow peas are resistant to disease and can be grown over a long season. The variety Oregon Sugar Pod II can be sown until July for a fall harvest.

Herbed Rice Salad

A DELICIOUS BOUQUET OF FRESHLY CUT *herbs gives this rice salad a bright taste. Be creative and try using different combinations of herbs, seeds, and nuts. Cashews, pine nuts, hazelnuts, and walnuts, toasted or raw, each lend a different character to the salad. While gathering sprigs of your favorite herbs, enjoy the sensual experience that can only come from your garden.*

¼ cup olive oil
2 tablespoons tarragon
   white wine vinegar
1 teaspoon Dijon mustard
1 teaspoon soy sauce or tamari
3 cups cooked, hot brown rice
1 small carrot, diced
1 small stalk celery, diced
1 small green bell pepper, diced
2 tablespoons minced
   fresh parsley
2 green onions, chopped

2 tablespoons sunflower seeds
2 tablespoons minced
fresh chives
1 tablespon minced fresh dill
1 tablespon minced fresh
   tarragon
1 tablespon minced fresh
   rosemary
red tomatoe wedges or
   slices of bell pepper, for
   garnish

In a large bowl, whisk together the olive oil, vinegar, mustard, and soy sauce or tamari. Add the hot rice, carrot, celery, green pepper, parsley, green onions, sunflower seeds, chives, dill, tarragon, and rosemary and mix well. Cover and refrigerate for at least 2 hours to allow the flavors to blend. Garnish with tomato wedges or red pepper slices. Best served at room temperature. Serves 4 to 6.

Chives are easy to grow if you give them rich, moist soil in a location at least half-sunny. They return each year bursting with fresh flavor in the spring. Those beautiful lavender blossoms not only are good for eating but are lovely as dried flowers. Divide the clumps and replant in fresh soil if they start to diminish in size. Because rust disease can be a problem, take care to destroy any plants that show signs of orange spotting on the leaves.

Purple Potato Salad

WHO BUT WE GARDENERS ever heard of eating purple potatoes? This wildly colorful dish makes for interesting conversation at potlucks. The French-style dressing offers a refreshing change from a more traditional potato salad.

> 5 cups peeled, cubed, and steamed purple potatoes
> 3 cups tomato wedges or whole cherry tomatoes
> 1 medium red onion, thinly sliced
> ½ cup chopped fresh parsley
> ½ to 1 cup dressing
> 3 hard-boiled eggs, sliced

DRESSING

> 1 large plum tomato, chopped
> 1 clove garlic, minced
> 1 green onion, finely chopped
> 1 teaspoon Dijon mustard
> 3 tablespoons red wine vinegar
> 1 teaspoon minced fresh oregano
> ¼ teaspoon salt
>
> ⅛ teaspoon freshly ground pepper
> ⅛ teaspoon cayenne pepper
> ¼ teaspoon sugar
> ¾ cup fresh tomato juice
> 1 tablespoon minced fresh parsley

In a large bowl, combine the thoroughly cooled potatoes with the tomatoes, onion, and parsley. To make the dressing, in a food processor, puree the tomato, garlic, and green onion. Add the mustard, vinegar, oregano, salt, pepper, cayenne pepper, and sugar and mix thoroughly. Slowly add the tomato juice, blending well. Stir in the parsley. Pour the dressing over the salad and toss gently. Add the eggs last so they don't crumble. Refrigerate before serving. Serves 8.

Red Potato Salad

THE FUN PART OF THIS RECIPE *is digging the fresh potatoes—a true treasure hunt. Finding them all is the challenge, but if a few elusive tubers suddenly appear in your garden next spring, you can have another round of potato salad.*

5 cups steamed red potato chunks
1½ cups diced cucumbers
¼ cup chopped green onions
½ medium red onion, thinly sliced
4 fresh mint leaves, minced

DRESSING
¾ cup yogurt
¾ cup sour cream
¼ cup minced fresh parsley
1 tablespoon minced fresh dill
2 cloves crushed garlic
2 teaspoons honey
½ teaspoon freshly
   ground pepper

In a large bowl, combine the potatoes, cucumbers, green onions, red onion, and mint leaves. In a medium bowl, mix all the dressing ingredients together. Pour over the vegetables, toss lightly and chill at least 2 hours before serving.
Serves 6 to 8.

New potatoes are the first maturing potatoes on the plant, ready to harvest when the flowers are fully opened. Carefully feel around the plant's base to see if the potatoes are the size of a large egg. Harvest a few, then hill the soil back up around the plant and continue to water evenly for more top-quality spuds.

Zesty Beet and Potato Salad

BLUE CHEESE AND HORSERADISH *provide the zip for this beet and potato salad. It was a hit with our recipe testers, even among those who claim to dislike beets and blue cheese.*

> 4 medium beets, cooked, peeled, and sliced
> 1½ cups cubed, cooked potatoes
> 1 cup diced red onions

DRESSING
> ½ cup crumbled blue cheese
> 4 teaspoons olive oil
> 1 teaspoon prepared horseradish
>   (see recipe under Horseradish Dip, page 174)
> 1 tablespoon minced fresh dill
> 1 clove garlic, minced
> salt to taste
> freshly ground pepper to taste

In a bowl, combine the beets, potatoes, and onions. To make the dressing, whisk together the blue cheese, olive oil, horseradish, dill, garlic, salt, and pepper. Pour over the vegetables and toss gently. Refrigerate at least 3 hours to commingle the flavors.
Serves 4.

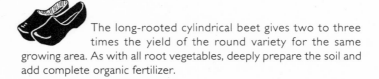

The long-rooted cylindrical beet gives two to three times the yield of the round variety for the same growing area. As with all root vegetables, deeply prepare the soil and add complete organic fertilizer.

Chilled Spaghetti Salad
with Garden Vegetables

SURPRISINGLY, LEFTOVER SPAGHETTI *makes an ideal base for vegetable and pasta salads. It is even worth boiling extra spaghetti on purpose for this red pepper and asparagus version. You can substitute green beans, purple beans, any color pepper, or whatever your garden has given you. There's also plenty of room for experimentation in choosing the vinegar; try adding the tarragon or basil flavored ones to your salad.*

2 large red bell peppers
1½ teaspoons olive oil
2 cloves garlic, minced
½ cup chopped fresh basil
3 cups asparagus, cut into 1-inch pieces
1 cup sliced mushrooms
¾ cup chopped fresh parsley
salt to taste
freshly ground pepper to taste
¼ cup red wine vinegar
8 to 10 ounces spaghetti, cooked

Roast the whole red peppers under the broiler, charring all sides. Cool in a paper bag before removing the skin. Clean out the seeds and center membrane and cut into bite-sized strips. Place the peppers in a large bowl and add the oil, garlic, and basil. Refrigerate for 30 minutes. In a saucepan, lightly steam the asparagus and mushrooms until the asparagus are barely tender, about 2 to 3 minutes. Add the vegetables to the red peppers, then add the parsley, salt, pepper, and vinegar. Mix together and toss with the spaghetti. Chill slightly before serving.
Serves 4.

Zucchini and Pesto Pasta Salad

THE HEIGHT OF SUMMER'S GLORY *is featured in this combination of young yellow and green squash, tomatoes, and basil. Next time you have a picnic, take along this salad; it travels well.*

6 ounces spiral pasta
2 cups sliced zucchini
2 cups sliced yellow squash
¹⁄₂ cup pine nuts
15 cherry tomatoes
¹⁄₂ cup finely grated fresh Parmesan cheese
1 cup Basil Pesto (page 142)
fresh whole basil leaves, for garnish

In a large pot, cook the pasta. Then drain, rinse, and cool. Steam the zucchini and yellow squash until just barely tender, about 2 to 4 minutes. Toast the pine nuts in a dry skillet or a 400° F oven until slightly brown. Toss the pasta, squash, pine nuts, and tomatoes with the cheese and pesto sauce. Chill before serving. Garnish with whole basil leaves.
Serves 10.

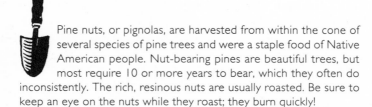

Pine nuts, or pignolas, are harvested from within the cone of several species of pine trees and were a staple food of Native American people. Nut-bearing pines are beautiful trees, but most require 10 or more years to bear, which they often do inconsistently. The rich, resinous nuts are usually roasted. Be sure to keep an eye on the nuts while they roast; they burn quickly!

Wild Rice and Parsley Salad

GATHER UP THE BOUNTY *of your cool-weather herbs for this flavorful wild and brown rice salad. It can be made as hot as a firecracker or as cool as evening dew. A cup of cilantro and another of parsley add crispness to the slightly chewy rice.*

4 cloves garlic, crushed
1 tablespoon toasted
   sesame oil
2 cups cooked brown rice
1 cup cooked wild rice

½ cup chopped celery
½ cup chopped red onions
1 cup minced fresh cilantro
1 cup minced fresh parsley

DRESSING
   ½ cup extra virgin olive oil
   juice of 1 lime
   2 tablespoons balsamic vinegar
   salt to taste
   hot red peppers to taste
   few sprigs of mint, basil, thyme, and other favorite herbs
   2 cups peeled, cooked shrimp (optional)

In a skillet sauté the garlic in the sesame oil over low heat until just tender. In a large bowl, mix the brown and wild rice, celery, onions, cilantro, and parsley. To make the dressing, whisk together the olive oil, lime juice, vinegar, salt, hot peppers, and herbs. Pour over the rice mixture and toss, adding the shrimp last, if used. Serves 6.

Two familiar parsley varieties are Italian flat-leafed and moss-curled. Used as a garnish, moss-curled is light to medium green, densely crinkled, and compact. The Italian flat-leafed is taller and has dark green leaves and a much more intense parsley flavor.

Fresh French Dressing

COLORFUL SALADS *that show off your hand-picked vegetables become even more rewarding when the homemade dressing begins with a juicy tomato, a tangy green onion, and a sprig of parsley, all from your garden. If you have made your own fresh tomato juice, all the better. Displayed in your fanciest bottle, it will give your friends yet another opportunity to admire your garden bounty.*

1/2 cup chopped tomatoes
1 clove garlic
1/2 cup chopped green onions
1 teaspoon Dijon mustard
3 tablespoons red wine vinegar
2 teaspoons minced fresh oregano
1/4 teaspoon salt
1/8 teaspoon freshly ground pepper
1/8 teaspoon cayenne pepper
1/4 teaspoon sugar
3/4 cup fresh tomato juice
1 tablespoon minced fresh parsley

In a food processor, puree the tomatoes, garlic, and onions. Add the mustard, vinegar, oregano, salt, pepper, cayenne pepper, and sugar and mix well. Add the tomato juice slowly, blending thoroughly. Before transferring the dressing into a bottle, gently stir in the parsley.
Makes 1 1/2 cups.

Balsamic Vinegar Dressing

CLASSIC OIL AND VINEGAR DRESSINg *becomes extraordinary when extra virgin olive oil is used. This dressing is especially nice over a salad of tender, nutty-flavored arugula and thin slices of crisp red onion.*

$\frac{1}{4}$ **cup extra virgin olive oil**
3 tablespoons balsamic vinegar
1 clove garlic, minced
$\frac{1}{4}$ **teaspoon grated lemon zest**
$\frac{1}{8}$ **teaspoon freshly ground pepper**
salt to taste
2 tablespoons minced fresh basil

In a small bowl, whisk together the olive oil, balsamic vinegar, garlic, lemon zest, pepper, and salt until smooth. Stir in the basil and transfer to a container with a tight-fitting lid. Shake well before serving.
Makes $\frac{1}{2}$ cup.

Berry Vinaigrette

A LITTLE OUT OF THE ORDINARY, *this rosy-red vinaigrette is easy to make and is exceptionally tasty on spinach salads. It's amazing how a little homemade jam can enhance a simple oil and vinegar dressing.*

> 1 tablespoon Dijon mustard
> ¼ cup seasoned rice or white wine vinegar
> 1 cup walnut oil
> 1 tablespoon raspberry or blackberry jam

In a small bowl, whisk the mustard with the vinegar and oil until a smooth consistency is reached. Add the jam and blend thoroughly. Transfer to a bottle and store in a cool dark place or refrigerate. Shake well before serving.
Makes 1¼ cups.

Low-Fat Dressing with Horseradish

THE HARDY PERENNIAL HORSERADISH, *with large floppy leaves and thick white roots, adds a sensational taste to this dressing. Fresh, dark green chives from the garden speckle the creamy whiteness with a subtle oniony flavor.*

> 1 cup low-fat cottage cheese or quark
> 1 cup nonfat yogurt
> 3 tablespoons snipped chives
> 2 tablespoons prepared horseradish
>   (see recipe under Horseradish Dip, page 174)

In a food processor, combine the cottage cheese or quark, yogurt, chives, and horseradish. When a smooth consistency is reached, transfer the dressing to a container and chill before serving.
Makes 2 cups.

Steamed, Sautéed, and Grilled Vegetables

I sort of missed the boat on taking care of my tomatoes. The slugs got to several big ones that were close to the ground. I don't know how many slugs I've dispatched since spring began. One day I was trying to get out of my garden without stepping on the onions when I slipped on a slug and fell flat on my back on the path. The lady who went to Paris—hers is the garden over by the big drain—came running over to see if I was okay. Very embarrassing! I said, "Oh, I slipped on a slug!"

—A Picardo farmer

Artichokes Filled
with Herbed Tomatoes

STEAMING HOT ARTICHOKES, *their centers filled and leaves packed with seasoned tomatoes, are attractive served on a bed of rice and garnished with parsley. Freshly harvested artichokes taste much better than store-bought and are so tender it's hard to believe they're the same vegetable.*

> 4 medium to large artichokes
> 1 cup chopped onions
> 2 tablespoons olive oil
> 1½ cups seeded, chopped tomatoes
> 4 tablespoons chopped fresh parsley
> salt to taste
> freshly ground pepper to taste
> 4 shallots, minced
> 1 tablespoon chopped fresh oregano

To prepare the artichokes, first cut off the stems. Next, snip off the thorny tips of the leaves. Pry apart the center and scrape out the choke, or hairy part, with a spoon. Stand the artichokes upright on a steamer and place the steamer over water in a deep pan with a lid.

In a bowl, combine the onions, oil, tomatoes, parsley, salt, pepper, shallots, and oregano and spoon into the center of each artichoke, placing the extra mixture between the outer leaves. Simmer the stuffed artichokes 30 to 45 minutes. Check occasionally to make sure there is sufficient water. Serve hot or at room temperature. Serves 4.

 The Pacific Northwest climate is not the best for reliable perennial artichoke plants. Arctic blasts and damp conditions are not favorable for their wintering-over, but growing the variety Green Globe as an annual will give you a nice harvest in August and September from spring-planted transplants.

Scallopini Squash Stars

WHEN SLICED HORIZONTALLY, *Scallopini squash are circular with a starlike wavy edge. Dark green, white, light green, or yellow, all scalloped squash are beautiful, especially when mixed together. For the best flavor, shape, and texture, pick them when they are 2 to 3 inches across.*

> **6 to 8 small Scallopini or other patty pan squash,**
> **thinly sliced horizontally**
> **2 tablespoons chopped fresh chives**
> **3 tablespoons butter, melted**
> **2 tablespoons toasted sesame seeds**

Steam the squash until just tender, about 2 to 4 minutes, and place in a warm serving dish. Toss the squash with the chives and butter. Garnish with the sesame seeds before serving.
Serves 2 to 4.

Manuring, fertilizing, and liming your soil are all good steps to take for growing healthy summer squash plants. Although squash can withstand dry conditions, the fruit will plump and the plants will produce more heavily if well watered. Be sure to keep water off the foliage to avoid diseases such as powdery and downy mildew. Some of the varieties available are the golden Sunburst, white patty pan, dark green Scallopini, and Benning's Green Tint.

Savory Savoy Cabbage

OUR TYPICAL WINTERS in the Pacific Northwest are ideal for growing Savoy cabbage, an elegant vegetable with a chartreuse heart and crinkly glaucous-blue outer leaves. Cabbage can have a soft or mushy texture when cooked, but here it retains its crispness and delicacy. Rich in nutrients, this "cooked coleslaw" is a most unusual way to use winter cabbage. Freshly grated horseradish is combined with honey and lemon juice in a warm, pungent dressing that brings comfort on a cozy winter evening.

> **3 cups shredded Savoy cabbage**
> **3 tablespoons butter, melted**
> **1 teaspoon fresh lemon juice**
> **1 teaspoon freshly grated horseradish**
> **freshly ground pepper to taste**
> **1 teaspoon honey**

Steam cabbage until crisp-tender, about 10 minutes. Drain and place in a serving dish. In a small bowl, whisk together the butter, lemon juice, horseradish, pepper, and honey. Pour the sauce over the cabbage, toss gently, and serve.
Serves 2 to 4.

Hardy winter cabbage is worth the effort come winter solstice when you serve it fresh from your garden. Sow the seeds of Savoys in May or early June to get the best-sized plant before fall. There are new hybrids and dependable old ones to choose from, some that are ready in October and others that don't fill out until January. Try a few different ones to outsmart the unpredictable winter weather.

Cauliflower with a Lemon Twist

FRESH LEMON JUICE GIVES CAULIFLOWER *a bright lift. To carry the lemon theme, adorn it with a sprinkling of lemon-gem marigold petals or lemon geranium blossoms. For an additional twist, infuse the broth with a lemon flavor from a bouquet of the many lemony herbs.*

4 cups cauliflower florets
2 tablespoons butter
2 tablespoons flour
½ cup Vegetable Broth (page 26)
salt to taste
freshly ground pepper to taste
juice of half a lemon

Steam the cauliflower until tender, 5 to 10 minutes. Set aside. In a saucepan, melt the butter; add the flour and lightly brown. Gradually stir in the broth and bring to a boil. Reduce heat and season with the salt, pepper, and lemon juice. Add the cauliflower and cook together for 1 minute. Serve hot. Serves 4.

Lemons don't grow well in Northwest gardens. Alternatives for our gardens are the various lemon-flavored herbs, such as lemon balm, lemon basil, lemon grass, lemon geranium, lemon thyme, and lemon verbena. Among all the choices, there will be one for your growing conditions.

Sesame Beans

GREEN BEANS GLISTEN in a bright sauce, a striking party presentation served on your whitest platter. Try using yellow or wax beans for a truly electric-colored dish. (Remember that turmeric can permanently stain porous or plastic serving pieces.) This dish is easy and spicy, but not pepper-hot.

> 6 cups green or yellow beans, trimmed
> 6 tablespoons toasted sesame oil
> 2 tablespoons sesame seeds
> ½ teaspoon ground turmeric
> 1 tablespoon sugar
> ½-inch piece fresh ginger, peeled and grated
> 1 tablespoon seasoned rice or cider vinegar
> calendula blossoms or sprigs of fresh basil, for garnish

Steam beans over boiling water for 5 minutes, until crisp-tender. In a large skillet, warm the oil over medium heat. When hot but not smoking, add the sesame seeds and sizzle until golden. Add the turmeric, sugar, and ginger, stirring the mixture as it cooks for 1 minute. Then add the beans and vinegar, mixing until lightly coated. Chill and arrange attractively on a serving platter or in a large bowl. Garnish green beans with calendula flowers, and yellow beans with sprigs of green or purple basil.
Serves 4.

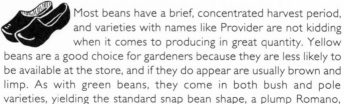 Most beans have a brief, concentrated harvest period, and varieties with names like Provider are not kidding when it comes to producing in great quantity. Yellow beans are a good choice for gardeners because they are less likely to be available at the store, and if they do appear are usually brown and limp. As with green beans, they come in both bush and pole varieties, yielding the standard snap bean shape, a plump Romano, and a rare type with a crescent moon curl. Yellow beans stand out among green leaves, making them easier to see when harvesting.

Spinach with Ginger

WE'RE ALL FAMILIAR WITH POPEYE, *the spinach-gulping cartoon char-*
acter who claimed super strength from canned greens. But Popeye
never had spinach that tasted this good! Braised fresh spinach cannot
be compared to canned. The flavor punch here comes from the toasted
sesame oil.

4 cups coarsely chopped spinach
1 tablespoon toasted sesame oil
1 clove garlic, minced
¼ teaspoon grated fresh ginger
1 tablespoon soy sauce or tamari
1 tablespoon sugar
1 tablespoon water

Wash the spinach thoroughly and set aside to drain. In a large
skillet, heat the oil, then add the garlic and ginger and cook until
lightly brown. Add the spinach, soy sauce or tamari, sugar, and
water. Cover and steam until the spinach is wilted, 1 to 3 minutes,
stirring once or twice. Remove cover and continue cooking on high
heat until the liquid is evaporated. Serve immediately.
Serves 4.

 Maritime gardeners can get a jump on next year's spring
spinach by starting hardy variety seedlings in late summer.
The spinach plant winters over best under a floating row
cover such as Reemay. This protects the plants and
encourages an earlier, more vigorous crop. A side dressing of
blood meal mixed into the soil in the spring next to the spinach
rosettes will break what is known as cold-soil lethargy and will help
you grow large, succulent, and tasty plants, ready for harvest before
spring has officially arrived.

Vegetable Curry

A SPIRITED BLEND of Middle Eastern spices makes the basic potato, tomato, and cabbage combination sensational.

3 tablespoons canola oil
2 teaspoons brown mustard seeds
2 teaspoons cumin seeds
2 teaspoons fenugreek seeds
1 onion, sliced
2 cloves garlic, chopped
2-inch piece fresh ginger, minced
1 teaspoon ground turmeric
2 teaspoons ground cumin
4 teaspoons ground coriander

1 cup water
3 cups chopped tomatoes
2 cups cubed potatoes
1 cup sliced carrots
3 cups shredded green cabbage
¼ cup shelled fresh peas
juice of half a lemon
salt to taste
chopped fresh cilantro, for garnish

In a large skillet with a lid, heat the oil and sauté the mustard, cumin, and fenugreek seeds, covering quickly until they stop popping. Add the onion, garlic, and ginger and sauté until the onion is translucent. Add the turmeric, cumin, and coriander and sauté for 1 minute. Remove this mixture from the heat and puree in a food processor with the water. Return to the pan and stir in the tomatoes, potatoes, and carrots. Cover and simmer for 8 minutes. Add the cabbage, cover, and simmer for 20 minutes. Then add the peas, lemon juice, and salt and mix well. Serve hot, garnished with fresh cilantro.
Serves 4 to 6.

Timing is crucial when planting a garden, as is the variety of the plant you choose. Early-maturing cabbage sown in March will make a summertime head, perfect for harvesting with your new potatoes and early-ripening tomatoes. A summer planting will give you a big crisp head for fall harvest.

Broccoli with Pine Nuts

ONE WINTER THE RAINS *were so heavy that Picardo Farm P-Patch was under 2 feet of water. We know for certain that broccoli is one of the most nutritious and delicious vegetables because the ducks didn't leave any of this hardy crop uneaten. Harvest your broccoli when the flower buds are tight and green to capture all the vitamins and minerals (A, B, C, calcium, and phosphorus) at their peak.*

    4 cups chopped broccoli
    1 tablespoon oil
    1 tablespoon butter
    juice of half a lemon
    ⅓ cup lightly toasted pine nuts

Steam the broccoli for 2 minutes and remove from heat. In a skillet, heat the oil, butter, and lemon juice. Add the broccoli and sauté for 3 minutes. Stir in the pine nuts and continue cooking for 2 minutes. Serve immediately.
Serves 4.

Broccoli plants need to be spaced 18 to 24 inches apart. For each broccoli plant, mix about ½ cup complete organic fertilizer into the planting hole. To avoid club root, a disease that affects plants of the cabbage family, keep records of your cole crop growing zones and rotate in three-year intervals, making sure to incorporate extra lime before planting.

Cajun Collards

TOMATOES AND PEPPERY-HOT CAJUN *flavors turn hearty collard greens into a full-bodied, zesty meal. These spicy greens are delicious served with seafood, rice, beans, sweet winter squash, or corn bread.*

10 medium collard leaves, stems removed
1 tablespoon oil
1 teaspoon cumin seeds
1 teaspoon mustard seeds
1 to 2 dried hot red peppers, crumbled
1 cup chopped onions
¼ cup cider vinegar
½ tablespoon sugar
2 cups chopped tomatoes

Slice the collard leaves into 1-inch strips and set aside. In a heavy skillet, heat the oil and add the cumin and mustard seeds, cooking until they sizzle and pop. Then add the hot peppers and onions. Continue cooking until the onions are soft but not brown. Mix in the collards, cider vinegar, and sugar, stirring often over medium heat for 20 minutes. Add tomatoes and simmer for 10 minutes. Serves 4.

Of all greens, collards have the highest calcium content, even more than in 1 cup of low-fat milk. Bok choy, kale, mustard, broccoli, and dandelion are also good sources. Calcium is best absorbed if you consume it with legumes, pumpkin seeds, buckwheat, fresh peas, or corn, which are all rich in phosphorus. Luckily, gardeners can grow all of these in the Pacific Northwest climate. Be sure to provide nutrients for your soil and plants in order to get a good return from the vegetables.

THE CITY GARDENER'S COOKBOOK

Coed Asparagus

ASPARAGUS IS GOOD *by itself, but this simple recipe adds a subtle, nutty flavor and is quick to make. Did you know asparagus is dioecious, having male and female flowers borne on separate plants? There is no taste difference between the "boys" and "girls," which you can distinguish when the plants are tall and ferny; the females produce vibrant red berries.*

20 spears asparagus
1 teaspoon oil
½ teaspoon toasted sesame oil
dash of soy sauce or tamari
freshly ground pepper to taste
toasted sesame seeds, for garnish

Snap off the tough ends of the asparagus and diagonally slice the more tender portions into 1-inch pieces. In a skillet, heat oils together until hot. Add the asparagus, soy sauce or tamari, and pepper. Cover and cook over high heat for 4 minutes, gently shaking to keep from sticking. Garnish with sesame seeds. Serves 2 to 4.

Asparagus is a perennial plant that becomes stronger after growing at least 3 years. The longer you wait, the stronger the plants will become. In established beds, discontinue harvesting by June to allow the plants to recover and gain strength for next year's crop. Asparagus roots in an exposed planting position can be loosened and taxed by strong winds, so consider supporting the plants for the rest of the growing season. It requires a thick layer of manure in the fall to help protect the tips from harsh winter weather. The manure provides nutrients in the spring when growth resumes.

Tomato Halves in Garlic Cream

THIS IS A SIMPLE YET ELEGANT side dish that warrants doubling the recipe to use more of your abundant tomatoes.

2 large tomatoes
1 tablespoon butter
1 clove garlic, halved
2 tablespoons cream
1 tablespoon minced fresh basil
salt to taste
freshly ground pepper to taste

Cut the tomatoes in half horizontally. In a skillet, melt the butter, add garlic, and sauté. Place the tomato halves cut side down and cook for 2 to 3 minutes, until tender but still holding their shape. Gently press the tomatoes to release a little juice. With a slotted spoon, transfer the tomatoes to a heated serving dish and keep warm. Remove the garlic from the pan and add the cream, basil, salt, and pepper. Cook until slightly thickened, about 5 minutes. Pour over the tomatoes and serve.
Serves 4.

 Before you plant, it is important to know what type of tomatoes you have. This aids in deciding whether or not to stake them, and how closely they can be planted to other crops. Check your seed source or ask when you buy your plants whether you have determinate or indeterminate plants. Determinate varieties grow to a set height and are usually bushy; the fruit ripens all at once, which is good for canning or freezing. Indeterminate varieties grow by climbing or sprawling to no particular height, and the fruit ripens over a long period.

THE CITY GARDENER'S COOKBOOK

Shredded Beets and Red Cabbage

MOST OF US COOK FRESH BEETS *the same few ways, but shredding them raw for a stir-fry presents an entirely new use of this sometimes overlooked vegetable. Beets and red cabbage are combined with onions, apple, and vinegar for a pleasant sweet-tart balance. Try this dish with golden beets and green cabbage for variety.*

2 tablespoons oil
6 cups shredded red cabbage
1 ½ cups peeled, shredded beets
1 medium red onion, thinly sliced
1 large apple, grated
⅓ cup cider vinegar
2 tablespoons brown sugar
¼ teaspoon ground allspice
salt to taste
freshly ground pepper to taste

In a large skillet, heat the oil and stir-fry the cabbage, beets, and onion over high heat, until the cabbage begins to wilt. Add the apple, vinegar, brown sugar, and allspice, cooking until the apples are hot, about 1 minute. Season with salt and pepper and serve hot. Serves 4.

Red cabbage should be grown more often for at least three good reasons: its beautiful waxy blue and shiny burgundy colors, its ability to stand harsh weather conditions, and its high vitamin and mineral content. Good news for hard-working gardeners! With attention to planting times, red cabbage can be harvested almost year-round in the maritime Northwest. Plant Ruby Ball in the spring for summer harvest and Meteor or Red Rodan in the summer for a winter and spring harvest.

Eggplant Sautéed with Garlic

IF YOU SUCCEED IN GROWING EGGPLANT, *you'll want to feature its flavor in this lightly seasoned recipe. This is delicious served over rice, sprinkled with sesame seeds. The smell of cooking garlic invites your loved ones to share the fruits of your labor in the garden.*

6 cups peeled, cubed eggplant

1 tablespoon salt

3 tablespoons olive oil

2 cloves garlic, chopped

2 tablespoons chopped fresh parsley

1 teaspoon freshly ground pepper

salt to taste

lemon wedges, for garnish

Sprinkle the eggplant with the tablespoon of salt and place in a colander to drain for about 30 minutes. Rinse and drain on a towel. In a skillet, heat the oil, add the garlic and eggplant, and sauté over medium heat for about 10 minutes, until almost soft. Add parsley, pepper, and salt, and continue cooking for another 3 to 4 minutes. Serve while hot with lemon wedges on the side.
Serves 6.

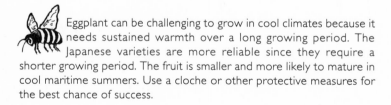 Eggplant can be challenging to grow in cool climates because it needs sustained warmth over a long growing period. The Japanese varieties are more reliable since they require a shorter growing period. The fruit is smaller and more likely to mature in cool maritime summers. Use a cloche or other protective measures for the best chance of success.

Green Beans
with Ginger and Fennel

THIS UNUSUAL COMBINATION *makes for an intriguing interplay of flavors and aromas.*

1 tablespoon butter
1 small onion, very thinly sliced
2 teaspoons minced fresh ginger root
2 tablespoons minced fennel leaves
salt to taste
40 tender green beans
¼ cup Vegetable Broth (page 26)

In a large skillet, heat the butter. Add the onion, ginger, fennel, and salt. Sauté until the onions are glazed and translucent, about 8 to 10 minutes. Add the whole beans and broth. Cover and cook until beans are just barely tender.
Serves 4.

Fennel is a beautiful perennial herb with aromatic, licorice-tinged leaves and seeds. Give fennel plenty of room and harvest the seeds promptly so that it doesn't become a nuisance next year. One plant produces an abundance of seeds. Ladybugs love the flat yellow flower heads of fennel. Please make sure you know how to identify ladybugs in all of their metamorphic stages. You'll want to protect them from harm since they love to eat aphids. Be aware that even many organically derived pesticides often kill beneficial insects as well as the destructive ones.

Mixed Greens
with Almonds and Basil

HERE'S A RECIPE *that gives you a chance to enjoy different garden greens such as spinach, beet tops, kale, and fresh basil. This makes a unique open-faced sandwich served on a warm, crusty bread with your favorite fancy mustard.*

2 tablespoons olive oil
1 cup sliced mushrooms
¼ cup sliced almonds
1 tablespoon chopped fresh basil
8 cups assorted greens, torn into pieces

In a large skillet, heat the oil and sauté the mushrooms, almonds, and basil. Wash the greens and place them dripping wet into the skillet. To avoid splattering, cover immediately with a tight lid. Cook for 2 minutes, then remove from heat and leave covered for 2 more minutes to finish steaming.
Serves 4.

Eat your thinnings! If you plant three rows of beets 6 inches apart, pull the middle row to use as greens and to provide space, light, and air for the remaining two rows. Then spread organic fertilizer down the middle; this makes a good side dressing for the remaining plants. Be sure to thin between the plants in each row as the beets grow. One beet every 5 inches is just about right.

THE CITY GARDENER'S COOKBOOK

Quick Zucchini

IT'S A TOSS-UP which takes longer, picking the fresh vegetables from the garden or fixing this simple family favorite.

2 tablespoons butter
2 cups grated zucchini
½ onion, chopped
chopped tomato (optional)

In a skillet, melt the butter, then add the zucchini and onion. Cook until tender, about 3 minutes, turning occasionally with a spatula. Add the tomato, if desired, and cook another 1 to 2 minutes. Serves 2 to 4.

The most important garden advice regarding zucchini is to harvest regularly. This productive plant comes in many colors other than green. Try the black, gray striped, yellow, and pale green varieties, but be forewarned: plant only one of each because they are naturally abundant.

Simply Great Carrots

BY GRATING AND QUICKLY COOKING *carrots you retain the flavor,
color, and vitamins. Simplicity is the key to this coarsely textured
carrot dish. The sweet, nutty taste blends well with walnuts and
raisins. For a holiday touch add whole cranberries.*

1 tablespoon butter
5 large carrots, coarsely grated
1 tablespoon water
freshly grated nutmeg to taste

In a skillet, heat butter until just bubbling. Add the carrots and
water and cook, covered, over low heat for 2 minutes. Gently turn
the carrots and cook 2 minutes more, uncovered. Sprinkle lightly
with nutmeg, stir well and serve.
Serves 4.

To prevent the loss of nutrients from your harvest, remember
that time, sunlight, and warm temperatures all take a toll on
vitamin content. Harvest in small amounts; keep the vegetables as
cool as possible when transporting; store in a cool, dark place;
and eat or preserve your pickings as soon as possible. Growing
the varieties bred for more vitamins will give you a nutritional advantage.
Among carrots, the varieties A+ and Mokum F1 have more vitamin A
than others.

THE CITY GARDENER'S COOKBOOK

Potatoes with Middle Eastern Spices

POTATOES ARE WONDERFULLY COMPATIBLE *with ethnic seasonings. Middle Eastern spices and cool, tart yogurt combine to make the "garden variety" potato an exotic dish.*

3 cups thickly sliced potatoes

2 tablespoons olive oil

½ cup chopped red bell peppers

1 cup chopped onions

1 tablespoon ground cumin

1 tablespoon ground coriander

⅛ teaspoon cayenne pepper

1 tablespoon butter, melted

⅓ cup chopped fresh cilantro

salt to taste

freshly ground pepper to taste

sour cream or yogurt (optional)

In a saucepan, steam the potatoes until just tender, about 5 to 8 minutes, and set aside. In a skillet, heat the oil and add the red peppers, onions, cumin, coriander, and cayenne pepper and cook until the onions begin to brown slightly. Stir in the potatoes and continue cooking until lightly browned. Remove the pan from the heat, spoon the potatoes into a bowl, drizzle with the melted butter, and sprinkle the cilantro, salt, and pepper over the top. Add a dollop of sour cream or yogurt, if desired.
Serves 4.

Potatoes, when exposed to the sun, develop green patches that indicate a high concentration of solanin just under the skin. To avoid ingesting the toxic ingredient, cut away any green pieces of the potato. Be warned that in the older heirloom varieties of potatoes, peeling off the green parts might not be sufficient to rid the potato of toxins, as generally is the case with the modern varieties. You may need to discard the whole potato. Keep soil hilled over the tubers and store them in a dark place to prevent greening.

Spinach Bhaji

HERE'S A TASTE OF THE MIDDLE EAST, *using garden greens exquisitely flavored with garlic, onion, and spices. Mixing mustard greens with the spinach adds a complementary flavor and is a good use for extra plants. Serve this over couscous, bulgur, or rice and top with crushed peanuts for extra crunch.*

½ teaspoon cumin seed, crushed
3 tablespoons olive oil
2 cloves garlic, minced
¼ cup chopped onions
8 cups chopped spinach
salt to taste
⅛ teaspoon cayenne pepper
1 tablespoon fresh lemon juice

In a hot, dry skillet, roast the cumin seed for 2 minutes to release the flavor. Add the oil, garlic, and onions, and sauté until the onion is tender. Stir in the spinach, season with salt and cayenne pepper, and stir continuously over high heat for 5 minutes. Mix in the lemon juice, remove from heat, and serve.
Serves 2 to 4.

 When hot weather takes hold, grow heat-resistant or summer varieties of spinach. Good choices are Mazurka, Olympia, and Steadfast. New Zealand spinach, not technically a spinach, will grow well in warm weather and reseeds year after year.

THE CITY GARDENER'S COOKBOOK

Sweet Corn Sautéed with Peppers

AFTER YOU'RE FILLED UP TO YOUR EARS *with corn on the cob, try this festive combination. Quickly sautéing the corn retains its splendid sweet flavor and crunch. Serve it with black beans for a protein complement and color contrast.*

> 2 tablespoons butter, divided
> 2 cups fresh corn kernels
> ¼ cup chopped red bell peppers
> ¼ cup chopped green bell peppers
> 1 tablespoon chopped onion
> 1 chopped cayenne or jalapeño pepper
> ¾ cup sour cream or yogurt

In a skillet, melt one tablespoon of the butter, add the corn, and sauté for 5 minutes. Stir in the remaining butter, red peppers, green peppers, onion, and cayenne or jalapeño. Cook for 5 minutes or until the peppers and onion are tender. Add the sour cream or yogurt and heat thoroughly, stirring constantly.
Serves 2 to 4.

 A carefully timed harvest of sweet corn yields peak flavor and texture. Pick corn when the kernels are plump and full of milky juice. The corn silk will be dry and brown and the cob filled out. The sugars start turning to starch quickly after harvest, so eat your corn as soon as possible for the sweetest flavor.

Baby Turnips
and Sweet Red Peppers

THOMAS JEFFERSON, *a most famous gardener, was able to choose from about 84 varieties of turnips in such colors as yellow, green, purple, orange, red, and black. This recipe features baby white turnips with sweet red peppers for color and simple seasonings that allow the sweetness of the young turnips to shine through. Imagine being able to pair orange turnips with green peppers or black turnips with yellow peppers.*

> 3 tablespoons butter
> 2 cups peeled, thinly sliced baby white turnips
> 2 red bell peppers, seeded and sliced
> 2 large cloves garlic, finely chopped
> salt to taste
> freshly ground pepper to taste

In a skillet, melt the butter. Add the turnips, red peppers, and garlic. Sauté over a moderate heat until the turnips are tender when pierced with a knife, but the peppers are still a bit crunchy. Season with salt and pepper.
Serves 2 to 4.

 Turnips taste especially good fresh from the garden. Here in the Northwest, they can be sown twice a year, in spring and in fall, even in poor soil. Both the leaves and the roots are edible and will grow unblemished under a floating row cover. Frost in the fall sweetens the flavor of the roots. A real challenge for the serious gardener would be to help seed-saving organizations preserve the many varieties of heritage seeds. Adopt an heirloom turnip and keep the remaining 25 or so varieties alive.

THE CITY GARDENER'S COOKBOOK

End-of-Vine Winter Squash Sauté

HMONG GARDENERS, *originally from the mountains of Laos, have given Northwest gardeners many new recipes for familiar plants. Tender new growth of most squash and bottle-gourd vines is often harvested while the rest of the plant continues to mature and produce. Use the newest 6 to 7 inches of squash vine tips in this recipe, and don't worry; the plant will sprout new shoots.*

4 cups winter squash vine tips
2 tablespoons oil
few uncooked squash blossoms, for garnish

Remove any tough threads from the squash vines. Wash and chop the vines into 1-inch pieces. In a skillet, heat the oil and stir-fry the vines until tender but still slightly crunchy.
Serves 4.

Cuisines from around the world call for various parts of plants that we do not always think of as edible. Besides the vine tips, the long-stemmed male squash blossoms are often used in soups or filled with cheese, dipped in egg, and fried for an appetizer. Many plants have one edible part and other parts that are toxic, such as tomato, potato, and rhubarb. In the case of jicama, a delicious tuber from a warmer climate, the immature seed pod is edible, but the leaves and the mature pods produce their own pesticide, rotenone.

Vietnamese-Style Lettuce Rolls

INSPIRED BY VIETNAMESE SPRING ROLLS, this recipe has stir-fried vegetables generously piled into the curved central leaves of cos or romaine. For a quick appetizer or side dish, the piping hot vegetables can be scooped into the lettuce, given a dash of peanut or other sauce, and eaten immediately. But if you want to present a platter that is a standout on the banquet table, cool the vegetables before filling the lettuce leaves, wrap the rolls with a ribbon of green onion tops cut into long strips, and secure with a toothpick. Adorn each roll with a small nasturtium leaf and decorate the platter with nasturtium flowers.

> 1 tablespoon toasted sesame oil
> 2 cloves garlic, pressed
> 1 peeled and julienned broccoli stalk
> 1 cup grated carrots
> 1 cup sliced green onions
> 4 egg whites, lightly beaten
> ½ cup sliced mushrooms
> 1 cup mung bean sprouts
> 1 8-ounce cake steamed teriyaki tofu, sliced into thin strips
> ¼ cup chopped fresh cilantro
> ½ teaspoon grated lemon or lime zest
> 1 tablespoon fish sauce or soy sauce
> 18 inner leaves of cos or romaine lettuce
> soy sauce or Thai Peanut Sauce (page 136), for dipping

In a wok or large skillet, heat the oil, add the garlic and broccoli and stir-fry for about 3 minutes. Add the carrots and onions and continue stir-frying for a few minutes. Pour the egg whites into the hot vegetables and stir gently for about 1 minute, until the egg whites are cooked. Add the mushrooms, mix gently, and remove from the heat. Stir in the bean sprouts, tofu, cilantro, lemon or lime zest, and the soy or fish sauce. For a buffet-style meal, place

the hot vegetables on a platter and give each person lettuce leaves and sauce to serve themselves. If serving cold, cool the filling, drain off any excess liquid, and assemble and garnish as described above. Chill before serving and provide a sauce alongside the platter.
Serves 6.

To grow lettuce year-round, choose the varieties carefully and plant the right amount at the right time. Look for catalogs that divide their seed offerings by season. Lettuce is ideal for intensive planting, allowing for constant harvest. Start by scissoring a few individual leaves from the young plants, then cut the larger leaves, or even the entire center from cutting lettuces. The center will resprout from the cut stem. Interplant and reseed heading varieties every couple of weeks for a continual harvest. Be creative and mix reds, greens, butterheads, romaines, and crispheads.

Asian Stir-Fry

STIR-FRYING FRESH BOK CHOY and Chinese broccoli in a rich toasted oil with garlic and soy sauce is all it takes to create a meal with an authentic and distinctive flavor. The trick is to have all the vegetables cut and organized in the order of cooking. Mix the cornstarch into the broth ahead of time so the entire process can go quickly. Have a batch of rice or noodles ready, and the meal is complete in short order.

1 tablespoon peanut oil
1 teaspoon toasted sesame oil
3 cloves garlic, crushed
1 carrot, thinly sliced diagonally
5 green onions, sliced diagonally
1 head bok choy, stems cut diagonally, green tops separated and sliced
3 cups chopped Chinese broccoli

1 tablespoon cornstarch
½ cup Vegetable Broth (page 26)
1 tablespoon soy sauce or tamari
2 tablespoons chopped peanuts

In a wok or curved-sided skillet, heat the peanut oil along with the sesame oil just to the smoking point. Add the garlic, carrot, and green onions and stir briskly for 1 minute. Add the bok choy stalks along with the broccoli. In a small bowl, mix the cornstarch into the broth. Continue stir-frying as you pour the cornstarch mixture into the vegetables, heat to boiling, and cook until the sauce becomes translucent. After a few minutes of stirring, add the bok choy greens and sprinkle in the soy sauce. The sauce should coat the vegetables and glisten. Remove from heat when the greens begin to wilt and add the chopped peanuts.
Serves 4 to 6.

Chinese mustard cabbage, or bok choy, also called white mustard cabbage, is like two vegetables in one. Both the round white stem and the dark green leaves are used extensively in Asian cooking. The dark green leaves are highly nutritious and can be picked individually from a large plant in the fall. *Gai lohn,* or Chinese broccoli has a distinctive flavor unlike regular broccoli and is not interchangeable.

Cauliflower with Asiago Cheese

THE SIMPLE BLENDING of fresh cauliflower and Asiago cheese is sure to convert even those who think they don't like cauliflower. For variety, broccoli or Romanesco can be substituted.

4 cups cauliflower florets
¾ cup freshly grated Asiago cheese
⅛ teaspoon paprika

Lightly steam the cauliflower and place in an ovenproof dish. Top with cheese and dust with paprika. Broil until the cheese begins to bubble.
Serves 4.

Rich, well-worked soil is needed to grow the weak-rooted cauliflower plant. Keep the growth rapid and continuous by fertilizing and watering evenly. As with broccoli, half a cup of complete organic fertilizer worked into the planting hole is essential. Floating row covers provide a barrier from the cabbage moth, whose caterpillar eats the above-ground parts, and the cabbage root fly maggot, which eats the roots. Plant overwintering varieties of cauliflower such as Purple Cape, Armada, or Maystar in July for a spring harvest.

Grilled Vegetables

PREPARING DINNER in an outdoor kitchen is a perfect way to end a sunshine-filled day of summertime activities. Cooked over hot coals, freshly harvested vegetables acquire a smoky flavor and give off a sensational aroma. Lightly coat them with oil, sprinkle with herbs, and give a quick few turns on the grill, and you'll have a platter piled high with sizzling vegetables. Throw a sprig of your favorite herb, such as rosemary or sage, onto the coals to add yet another subtle flavor.

¼ cup olive oil
2 cloves garlic, crushed
salt to taste
minced fresh herbs to taste
assorted vegetables:
  zucchini or other summer squash, sliced in half lengthwise
  eggplant, sliced into ½-inch rounds or lengthwise
  whole green onions, scallions, or tender young leeks
  potatoes, quartered and precooked until almost tender
  whole tomatoes
  corn on the cob, shucked
  winter squash, precooked and sliced into wedges
  mushrooms

Pour the olive oil into a shallow bowl and mix in the garlic, salt, and herbs. Toss the vegetables in the oil to coat them lightly and grill on a hot fire for about 2 to 3 minutes per side. The vegetables can also be cut into bite-sized pieces and skewered for kabobs. Allow two 8-inch skewers per person.

 Periods of drought are stressful to plants and can trigger bolting of lettuce, broccoli, and cabbages and create hard rings in beets. Hollow heart in potatoes occurs when heavy rains or watering follows dry periods. This pattern can also cause tomatoes to crack. All your plants will benefit if you work humus into the garden beds to help retain water and maintain an even amount of moisture.

Casseroles
and Baked Vegetables

I wanted to take a few moments and say thanks for offering
this wonderful program. My partner is nearing the end of a long and
valiant struggle with AIDS. My P-Patch has been more
valuable during this experience than any counselor or support group.
It's marvelous to be there alone during the middle of the day—just me
and the insects—and have the time to reflect on our five-year
relationship. Or being able to take my anger out on unruly weeds or
clayish dirt clods. Or being able to work on something without having to
think at all. Amidst this death process that surrounds me I have this
little island of renewal and life. What a marvelous gift!

— A Burke Gilman gardener

Asparagus-Spoked Carrot
and Nut Casserole

THE CREATIVE COOK *likes to impress diners waiting at the table.
This casserole will show off your precious asparagus, arranged like the
spokes of a wheel, in a healthy style. The toasted seeds, orange zest,
and cilantro offer a lively, well-balanced taste. Sharp Cheddar and
walnuts create a tangy version, while Gruyère and pecans will be
milder.*

½ cup diced onions

¼ cup olive oil

4 cups shredded carrots

¼ cup chopped fresh cilantro

3 eggs, beaten

¾ cup toasted sesame seeds,
   divided

¼ cup grated sharp Cheddar
   or Gruyère cheese

½ teaspoon minced fresh
   rosemary

¼ teaspoon grated
   orange zest

½ teaspoon salt

12 asparagus spears,
   lightly steamed

¼ cup finely chopped
   walnuts or pecans

¼ cup finely chopped
   sunflower seeds

Preheat oven to 350° F. In a skillet, sauté the onions in the oil until
tender. Transfer the onions to a large bowl and add the carrots,
cilantro, and eggs. Stir in ½ cup of the sesame seeds, the cheese,
rosemary, orange zest, and salt. Spread this mixture in a lightly
greased 10-inch pie pan. Arrange the asparagus spears in a spoke
formation on top. In a small bowl, combine the chopped nuts, sunflower seeds, and remaining sesame seeds. Sprinkle this mixture
over the asparagus layer and bake, uncovered, for 45 minutes.
Serves 6.

Company Carrots

THERE IS NOTHING quite like pulling fresh carrots from your garden and brushing off the brown soil to reveal the bright orange roots. Julienned carrots, nestled like slender pick-up sticks in a shallow serving dish, drizzled with a smooth white sauce, and flecked with chopped green onion are a perfect dish for company.

4 cups julienned carrots
¼ cup water or reserved cooking liquid
½ cup mayonnaise
2 tablespoons finely minced onion
1 tablespoon prepared horseradish
(see recipe under Horseradish Dip, page 174)

salt to taste
freshly ground pepper to taste
¼ cup fine dry bread crumbs
2 tablespoons butter
¼ cup chopped fresh parsley
paprika, for garnish

Preheat oven to 375° F. In a covered saucepan, steam the carrots until barely tender, about 3 minutes. Arrange the carrots in an 8-inch greased baking dish. In a small bowl, mix ¼ cup water or reserved cooking liquid with the mayonnaise, onion, horseradish, salt, and pepper and pour over the carrots. In a separate bowl, combine the bread crumbs, butter, and parsley and spread evenly over the carrots. Garnish with the paprika. Bake, uncovered, for 10 to 15 minutes until toasted on top.
Serves 4.

 It is easy to sow carrot seeds too thickly, and many remedies have been suggested. To help you sow them more evenly, mix the seed with sand or a little dry soil before planting. Carrot seed is also available in pellet form or in strips of seed tape. The seeds take about 3 weeks to germinate, so be patient and remember to keep the soil surface moist. Thin carrot seedlings to about 1 inch apart. They will need to be thinned once more, but wait until they become baby carrots for thinnings that are a real taste treat.

Creamy Rutabaga Casserole

LONG BEFORE *refrigeration, winter-stored root crops like rutabaga were a staple of people in harsh northern lands such as Finland, where this recipe originated. Despite modernization, this delicious recipe continues to be passed from one generation to the next. At a harvest-time gathering of P-Patch gardeners this rich, mellow puree was consumed joyfully. If your cooked rutabagas turn out not to be very sweet, some honey may be added.*

4 medium rutabagas, peeled and diced

2 eggs, beaten

¼ cup cream

½ teaspoon freshly grated nutmeg

1 teaspoon salt

¼ cup dry bread crumbs

3 tablespoons butter

Preheat oven to 350° F. Steam the rutabaga until tender, about 30 minutes. When soft, mash and set aside. In a separate bowl, stir together the eggs, cream, nutmeg, and salt. Add the bread crumbs and mix well. Combine the egg mixture with the mashed rutabaga and place in a buttered 2½-quart casserole. Dot with butter and bake for about an hour until lightly browned. Serves 5.

Rutabaga, a sturdy yellow-fleshed root crop, is a cross between a turnip and a cabbage. It is fast growing, so a well-fertilized soil with extra lime is important. Cover the rutabagas with a floating row cover throughout the growing season to keep root maggots from damaging the crop. If you plan to keep the plants in the ground for winter storage, make sure the soil drains well to prevent rot. For perfect-sized roots, sow the seeds by mid-July; any earlier will result in huge woody roots, and any later may result in no roots at all. Each strain has its own assets. Look for one that will be sweet for this casserole, such as Stokes' Atlasweet from Canada.

Herbed Potato and Onion Bake

FRESHLY SNIPPED PARSLEY *and arugula provide the difference in this variation of scalloped potatoes, which should be considered a springboard for experimentation with other herbs. Another nice combination is dill and sorrel.*

3 cups chopped Walla Walla
   sweet onions
3 cloves garlic, minced
1 tablespoon olive oil
6 cups grated potatoes
1 tablespoon flour
½ teaspoon salt
⅛ teaspoon freshly
   ground pepper

1 teaspoon minced fresh
   thyme
¼ cup minced fresh
   parsley
¼ cup minced fresh
   arugula
1 egg
½ cup milk
¼ cup grated Jarlsberg

Preheat oven to 400° F. In a large skillet, sauté the onions and garlic in the oil until softened. Remove from heat and cool. Add the potatoes, flour, salt, pepper, thyme, parsley, and arugula and mix together. In a small bowl, lightly beat the egg; stir in the milk and pour over the potato mixture. Pour into a greased 2½-quart casserole. Sprinkle with the grated cheese and bake for 45 minutes.
Serves 6 to 8.

The famous Walla Walla sweet onions are a big, juicy variety named after the town in Eastern Washington where they are grown. Start with transplants rather than seeds for an early, reliable harvest. Remember that all onions require evenly moist soil throughout their growing season. This variety doesn't store well, so enjoy them while they're fresh.

Cheesy Vegetable Casserole

THIS TASTY STRATA OF SUMMER vegetables requires a little extra work to prepare, but the results are rewarding. If you choose to assemble this casserole the night before, you will have the luxury of simply baking it and serving a warm fresh bread on the side the next day. This is a good way to use a variety of garden vegetables and herbs.

1 medium eggplant,
  sliced into ½-inch rounds
1 cup diced potatoes
1 cup dry bread crumbs or
  Herbed Bread Crumbs (page 164)
2 tablespoons chopped fresh basil
2 tablespoons chopped fresh parsley
3 eggs, lightly beaten
½ teaspoon salt
freshly ground pepper to taste

1 medium zucchini,
  sliced
4 medium tomatoes,
  sliced
3 tablespoons olive oil
1½ cups grated
  mozzarella cheese
1 cup freshly grated
  Parmesan cheese

Preheat oven to 400° F. Place the eggplant slices on a greased baking sheet, cover with foil, and bake for 40 minutes. Remove from the oven and reduce heat to 375° F. Steam the potatoes until just tender, about 5 to 7 minutes, and let cool. In a small bowl, mix together the bread crumbs, basil, and parsley. In another bowl, combine the eggs with the salt and pepper. Oil a 9-by-13-inch baking dish and coat the bottom and sides with ¼ cup of the bread-crumb mixture. Layer the vegetables in the casserole, starting with the eggplant and continuing with the potato, zucchini, and finally the tomatoes. Sprinkle a portion of the egg mixture, olive oil, bread-crumb mixture, Parmesan, and mozzarella over each layer. Bake, covered, at 375° F for 45 minutes.
Serves 8 to 10.

Parsnip Flan

OFTEN UNDERRATED, *fresh parsnips have a mild, celerylike fragrance and a sweet, nutty flavor. Served on a bed of greens and garnished with red pear slices, this elegant flan is ideal for company.*

  3 cups peeled, sliced parsnips
  1 cup chopped onions
  2 tablespoons butter
  ½ cup Vegetable Broth (page 26)
  ½ cup milk
  2 eggs
  ¼ teaspoon freshly grated nutmeg
  freshly ground pepper to taste

Preheat oven to 350° F. In a large skillet, combine the parsnips, onions, butter, and broth. Simmer over low heat for 10 minutes. Puree the mixture with the milk, eggs, nutmeg, and pepper. Pour the puree into four custard cups and place them in an oven-proof dish filled with 1 inch of water. Cover tightly. Bake for 20 to 25 minutes, until set. Serve in custard cups or let stand for 3 minutes before removing from the custard cups by inverting onto a plate. Serves 4.

As with carrots, parsnips should be grown under a floating row cover, such as Reemay, to prevent carrot rust fly damage to the roots. Keep your parsnips covered for the entire growing season for best results. A crop sown in early July will yield parsnips throughout the winter.

Spinach and Rice
with Feta Cheese

THIS CLASSIC BLEND OF SPINACH, *brown rice, and cheese makes a wholesome main meal in spring or fall. The Northwest's climate, with a long, cool spring and mild fall, is ideal for growing large and tasty spinach plants.*

> 6 cups chopped fresh spinach
> 2 cups cooked brown rice
> ³⁄₄ cup feta cheese, cut into ¹⁄₄-inch cubes
> 1 egg
> 2 tablespoons chopped fresh parsley
> ¹⁄₄ teaspoon freshly ground pepper
> 1 tablespoon butter
> 2 tablespoons wheat germ

Preheat oven to 350° F. In a bowl, mix together the spinach, rice, and cheese and set aside. Beat the egg in a small bowl and add the parsley and pepper. Combine the egg and spinach mixtures and transfer to a greased 2-quart casserole. Dot the top with butter, then sprinkle with the wheat germ. Bake for 20 to 25 minutes.
Serves 4.

Is your spinach a summer or winter variety? These annual plants are day-length sensitive, which determines when the seed is to be sown. Hot and dry conditions trigger both types to bolt or go to seed. To prevent bolting, provide shade by sowing the round seeds of the summer varieties in early spring between taller crops. Harvest up to half of the leaves when they are good sized. Sow the prickly seeds of the winter varieties in a sunny spot in late summer. Harvest the leaves more sparingly throughout the fall and winter.

Squash, Tomato, and Onion Casserole

THIS IS A SPLENDID DISH for the late summer harvest, light on calories and easy on the cook. With only a brief stop at the cutting board between garden and oven, you'll have more time to play in the garden.

2 cups sliced zucchini
1 cup thinly sliced yellow crookneck or straightneck squash
1½ cups thinly sliced tomatoes
½ cup thinly sliced onions
1 tablespoon butter
1 tablespoon freshly grated Parmesan cheese
¼ cup chopped fresh parsley
12 fresh basil leaves
½ teaspoon grated lemon zest
salt to taste
freshly ground pepper to taste

Preheat oven to 350° F. Arrange sliced zucchini and yellow squash in a single layer in a shallow 1½-quart casserole, overlapping the slices. Top with a layer of the sliced tomatoes. Separate the sliced onions into rings and place over the tomatoes. Dot the vegetables with butter, then sprinkle with the Parmesan, parsley, basil, lemon zest, salt, and pepper. Bake until the vegetables are tender, about 20 minutes. Serves 4.

Yellow crookneck summer squash is an old favorite, grown in gardens season after season not for its looks but for its exceptional flavor. Harvest with a sharp knife because the twist and tear method used to harvest straightneck squash will usually break the crook of the neck.

Classic Spaghetti Squash

UNIQUE VEGETABLE *"noodles" with a slightly crunchy texture, accented with freshly minced parsley and basil, are served in the squash shell. How many cooks can claim to have grown the serving dish as well as the ingredients?*

> 1 large spaghetti squash
> 2 to 3 cloves garlic, pressed
> 4 tablespoons butter
> 1 cup freshly grated Parmesan cheese
> ¼ cup minced fresh parsley
> ¼ cup minced fresh basil
> salt to taste
> freshly ground pepper to taste

Preheat oven to 350° F. Slice the spaghetti squash in half. Scoop out the seeds, invert on a flat baking dish and bake until tender, about 30 minutes. While the squash is cooking, sauté the garlic in butter over low heat, until tender, and set aside. Remove the squash from the oven. While holding each half with a pot holder, scrape out the pulp with a fork into a large bowl. Add the garlic and butter, cheese, parsley, basil, salt, and pepper, and gently combine. Fill the squash shells with the seasoned "spaghetti" and serve immediately.
Serves 4.

Spaghetti squash is grown and stored like any winter squash. Protected by a hard shell, it has a much longer life span than summer squash. It is an especially good choice for children, who love to grow "spaghetti." The squash are rampant growers, producing an abundant crop and spreading far and wide. Be sure to leave them lots of room to sprawl. Your spaghetti "dishes" can be artfully decorated by scratching a design into the shell of the young, developing squash. As the vegetable grows, the scratches will callous over and enlarge.

Garden Burgers

THESE VEGETARIAN BURGERS *are tasty with traditional hamburger condiments or with other toppings, such as curried yogurt. Packed with vegetables and herbs, they add plenty of nutrition to your diet. Try different combinations of peppers, herbs, and cheeses.*

½ cup grated carrots
½ cup finely chopped celery
2 tablespoons finely chopped onion
¼ cup chopped green bell peppers
2 eggs, beaten
1 tablespoon oil
¼ cup fresh tomato juice

1 cup ground sunflower seeds
2 tablespoons wheat germ
2 tablespoons minced fresh parsley
1 tablespoon minced fresh oregano
1 tomato, sliced
½ cup grated cheese

Preheat oven to 350° F. In a medium bowl, combine the carrots, celery, onion, and green peppers. Add the eggs, oil, and tomato juice, mixing together until thoroughly moistened. Stir in the sunflower seeds, wheat germ, parsley, and oregano. Mix well and shape into patties. Arrange them in a greased shallow baking pan and bake until brown, about 15 minutes on each side. Top each burger with a slice of tomato and sprinkle with the grated cheese. Broil quickly to melt the cheese.
Makes 6 burgers.

VARIATIONS
hot peppers, cilantro, and jack cheese
red bell peppers, basil, oregano, and fresh mozzarella
green bell peppers, caraway seeds, and Swiss cheese

Baked Parsnip Fries

EVERYONE IS FAMILIAR with French fries, but how many people have made their own? The simple choice of baking rather than frying makes this version much healthier. Parsnips, a hardy root vegetable similar to carrots, are a good choice for those who desire a creative twist to the standard potato version. But don't stop there, pick those extra squash, carrots, potatoes, even salsify or Hamburg parsley, to create your own wonderful medley of "fries." Your choice of oil will make a big difference in taste, too. We suggest extra virgin olive oil, walnut oil, or hot pepper oil.

> **6 medium parsnips, peeled**
> **2 tablespoons oil**
> **salt to taste**

Preheat oven to 400° F. Cut parsnips lengthwise into French fry–like sticks. Brush lightly with oil and bake on cookie sheets. Turn with a metal spatula when brown and continue cooking until parsnip sticks become crispy on the outside and soft on the inside, about 30 to 45 minutes. Sprinkle with salt.
Serves 4.

Hamburg is a variety of parsley with edible, parsniplike roots. The cultivar, *Petroselinum crispum* var. *tuberosum,* has the advantage of being able to grow in low-light gardens, perfect for planting between rows or in the shade of berry bushes. Sow the seed in April; thin seedlings to 9 inches apart; and keep evenly watered. The roots will be ready for lifting in November. Harvest the leaves all season like any parsley, but use a little less because the taste is stronger. If peeled, the roots should be sprinkled with lemon juice before cooking to avoid discoloration.

Glazed Summer Carrots

COAT YOUR NEWLY HARVESTED *carrots with a shimmering glaze that is as bright as the summer sunshine.*

4 cups julienned carrots
6 green onions, chopped
4 tablespoons butter
1 tablespoon honey
1 tablespoon grated lemon zest
juice of half a lemon
salt to taste
freshly ground pepper to taste

Preheat oven to 350° F. In a covered saucepan, steam carrots until just tender, about 2 to 4 minutes. Place in an ovenproof dish and sprinkle with the green onions. Melt the butter in a small saucepan and add the honey, lemon zest, lemon juice, salt, and pepper. Simmer for 2 to 3 minutes, pour over carrots and green onions, and bake for 15 minutes.
Serves 4.

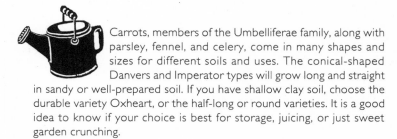

Carrots, members of the Umbelliferae family, along with parsley, fennel, and celery, come in many shapes and sizes for different soils and uses. The conical-shaped Danvers and Imperator types will grow long and straight in sandy or well-prepared soil. If you have shallow clay soil, choose the durable variety Oxheart, or the half-long or round varieties. It is a good idea to know if your choice is best for storage, juicing, or just sweet garden crunching.

Roasted Potatoes
with Sweet Red Peppers

A RED BELL PEPPER *is simply a green bell pepper that has been left on the vine to reach maturity. Red peppers are sweeter than green ones, easier to digest, have one and a half times as much vitamin C, and eleven times as much beta carotene. Long, bright strips of red peppers not only contribute to a healthy diet but make for an especially appealing dish when combined with white, blue, and yellow potatoes just dug from the earth.*

4 cups cubed potatoes
2 red bell peppers, seeded
    and cut into 1-inch strips
2 cloves garlic, minced
1½ cups coarsely
    chopped onions
2 green onions, chopped
2 tablespoons minced fresh
    oregano
2 tablespoons minced fresh
    marjoram
2 tablespoons minced
    fresh rosemary
½ teaspoon salt
½ teaspoon freshly
    ground pepper
½ cup olive oil

Preheat oven to 375° F. In a large bowl, combine the potatoes, red peppers, garlic, onions, and green onions. In a small bowl, whisk the oregano, marjoram, rosemary, salt, and pepper into the olive oil. Pour over the potato mixture and toss gently. Distribute evenly in a greased 9-by-13-inch baking pan. Bake for 40 minutes, turning once or twice.
Serves 6.

Potatoes, comparatively inexpensive in the store, are sometimes thought to be a waste of space for the home gardener, but newly harvested potatoes taste so much better. Potatoes can have a five-fold greater crop yield than that of corn or wheat in comparable growing space, not to mention the nutritional advantage of the spud. Vitamins are lost when potatoes are stored, which is another good reason to grow and harvest your own.

THE CITY GARDENER'S COOKBOOK

Pumpkin, Potato, and Ginger Gratin

WHEN CRISP FALL DAYS entice you to the garden, harvest bright orange pumpkins and tender cilantro leaves. Seasoned with lots of fresh ginger, this fragrant combination of spices and garden vegetables perfumes the kitchen with a sweet, earthy aroma.

6 cups cubed pumpkin
2 cups cubed potatoes
1 cup chopped onions
1 clove garlic, minced
2 tablespoons grated fresh ginger
1 teaspoon ground cumin
5 cardamom pods

6 tablespoons olive oil
juice of half a lemon
1¼ cups yogurt
salt to taste
chopped fresh cilantro,
   for garnish

Steam the pumpkin and potatoes together until just tender and set aside. In a skillet, sauté the onions, garlic, ginger, cumin, and cardamom in the oil until the onions are soft. Add the pumpkin and potatoes and cook until they are slightly brown. Stir in the lemon juice, yogurt, and salt, heating until warmed through. Transfer the mixture to a shallow ovenproof dish and broil until the surface is crisp. Garnish with chopped cilantro.
Serves 6.

In other countries any big orange squash is called a pumpkin. Many people only think of them as the blue ribbon–winning mammoths at the fairs. To have good tasty orange squash, choose varieties of pumpkins selected for cooking, such as Small Sugar or White Rind Sugar. The flavor varies with the specific variety and growing conditions. Bitterness can result if the plants suffer drought.

Spaghetti Squash
with Tomatoes and Feta Cheese

VEGETABLE SPAGHETTI, or *spaghetti squash*, *is a winter-stored squash with the unusual feature of interior meat that, when cooked, pulls out in strands similar to spaghetti. Try to grow the orange variety; it has more beta carotene than the yellow.*

  1 medium spaghetti squash
  1 cup chopped onions
  1 clove garlic, minced
  1 tablespoon oil
  1½ cups chopped tomatoes
  2 tablespoons chopped fresh cilantro
  ¾ cup crumbled feta cheese
  1 tablespoon chopped black olives
  ½ to 1 pound peeled, cooked shrimp (optional)

Preheat oven to 350° F. Cut the squash in half, scoop out the seeds, and invert onto a baking sheet. Bake the squash until tender, about 30 minutes. When cool enough to handle, scrape out the "noodles" with a fork and place on a serving platter. Keep warm. In a skillet, sauté the onions and garlic in the oil until the onions are translucent. Add the tomatoes and simmer for 5 minutes. Just before serving, stir in the cilantro, feta cheese, olives, and shrimp, if used. Pour the vegetables and shrimp over the spaghetti squash "noodles" and serve. Serves 4 to 6.

Spaghetti squash plants need warm growing conditions and a long summer season. As with other squash, prepare the soil, add manure, and keep plants well watered. To prevent disease, avoid water on the foliage. Squash should mature on the vine and be stored in a cool place. Harvest carefully to prevent bruising and leave a couple of inches of stem on the fruit for longer storage.

Mixed Vegetable Bhaji

*IF YOU LIKE TO SLICE, DICE, CUBE, AND SNAP, this recipe's for you!
The pungent spiciness of Indian seasonings melds the wide variety of
ingredients into a robust stew. It was a big hit at the annual P-Patch
harvest banquet, and is a banquet in itself. Serve with puris, an Indian
bread, or basmati rice. Garam masala, a mixture of cinnamon, cardamom, cloves, and other spices, is found in Indian specialty shops.*

2 cups sliced zucchini	2½ teaspoons *garam masala*
1½ cups peeled, cubed eggplant	2 teaspoons ground
2 cups cauliflower florets	coriander
3 cups peeled, cubed yams	3 teaspoons ground cumin
1 cup snap peas	1 tablespoon sugar
2 cups cubed potatoes	3 teaspoons paprika
1 cup diced carrots	1 teaspoon hot red
1 cup snapped green beans	pepper flakes
2 bananas, sliced	¾ teaspoon ground turmeric
½ cup ground sesame seeds	2 cloves garlic, minced
½ cup unsweetened	2 teaspoons salt
shredded coconut	¾ cup oil
½ cup ground roasted peanuts	¼ cup water

Preheat oven to 400° F. In a large bowl, combine the vegetables
and the bananas and set aside. In a separate bowl, mix together the
sesame seeds, coconut, peanuts, *garam masala*, coriander, cumin,
sugar, paprika, red pepper, turmeric, garlic, and salt. Add the spice
mixture a little at a time to the vegetables, mixing well. Arrange
them in a 9-by-13-inch baking pan, heat the oil and pour over the
vegetables. Then sprinkle with the water. Bake, covered, for about
1 hour, until the vegetables are tender.
Serves 8 to 10.

Roasted Winter Vegetables

WARM AWAY WINTER'S CHILL *with this hearty vegetable roast. Mix and match your favorite vegetables to vary the dish for different occasions, but always include the soy sauce, vinegar, and generous amounts of garlic.*

    2 tablespoons olive oil
    4 cups of any of the following cut into chunks: potatoes,
        turnips, rutabagas, beets, winter squash, onions,
        or sweet potatoes
    2 cups of any of the following cut into chunks: carrots,
        fennel, peppers, blanched cauliflower, or leeks
    10 whole cloves garlic
    soy sauce or tamari to taste
    freshly ground pepper to taste
    1 cup sliced mushrooms
    1 tablespoon vinegar
    cayenne pepper to taste

Preheat oven to 375° F. Spread the oil into a 9-by-13-inch baking pan. Add the first set of vegetables to the oil, toss to coat and bake for 15 minutes. Remove from the oven and stir in the second set of vegetables and the garlic. Sprinkle with the soy sauce or tamari and pepper, then bake for 15 minutes. Stir in the mushrooms, vinegar, and cayenne pepper and bake 5 minutes. Serves 4.

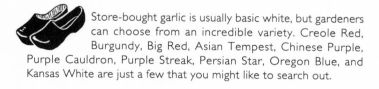

Store-bought garlic is usually basic white, but gardeners can choose from an incredible variety. Creole Red, Burgundy, Big Red, Asian Tempest, Chinese Purple, Purple Cauldron, Purple Streak, Persian Star, Oregon Blue, and Kansas White are just a few that you might like to search out.

Caramelized Onions in Winter Squash

PUNGENT ONIONS, *sweetened and cooked slowly, complement the mild, golden flesh of winter squash. Enjoy the vast variety of small squash such as acorn, Kuta, Danish, or Sweet Dumpling, all of which are appropriate for this dish. Each one offers its own taste and texture.*

2 small winter squash, halved and seeded
3 tablespoons brown sugar
4 cups chopped yellow onions
2 tablespoons butter
½ teaspoon grated orange zest

Bake the squash inverted on a baking sheet at 350° F until tender, about 30 to 40 minutes. In a heavy skillet, heat the sugar over low heat until melted, stirring until syrupy. Add the onions, butter, and orange zest. Cook about 8 minutes, until the onion mixture is caramelized. Spoon into the hot squash and serve immediately. Serves 4.

 It is tempting to save seeds from a particularly tasty squash with the idea of growing it again next year, but unless the flowers were hand pollinated, you'll probably be disappointed. Thanks to the bees, if you grow different varieties of summer and winter squash, pumpkin, or even gourds, cross-pollination is likely. Although probably edible, next year's hybrids will not taste the same, but then, having a pucchini or a zumpkin to carve into a jack-o'-lantern is at least out of the ordinary!

Emerald-Stuffed Tomatoes

GREEN PLANTS FLOURISH *in the maritime Northwest year-round. The extensive assortment of edible greens that do well here allows the gardening cook to take advantage of this bounty and prepare the choicest meals. Endive is the classic European green we suggest for this recipe, but arugula, sorrel, parsley, radicchio, cress, and mustard each lend a distinctive flavor.*

4 cloves garlic, minced
1 cup chopped onions
2 tablespoons olive oil
3 cups finely chopped greens
4 whole tomatoes
⅛ teaspoon freshly
   ground pepper
1 tablespoon red wine vinegar

1 cup dry bread crumbs or
   Herbed Bread Crumbs
   (page 164)
½ cup grated Cheddar cheese
¼ cup freshly grated
   Parmesan cheese
½ cup ground walnuts

Preheat oven to 325° F. In a large skillet, sauté the garlic and onions in the olive oil until tender. Add the greens, stir, and remove from the heat. Hollow out the tomatoes by scraping out the seeds, pulp, and juice with a spoon. Add the tomato pulp, pepper, and vinegar to the greens. Return to heat and simmer until the juice from the tomatoes evaporates. Remove from the heat and stir in the bread crumbs, half of the Cheddar, the Parmesan, and nuts. Fill the tomatoes with the warm stuffing and top with the remaining Cheddar. Bake in a greased 8-by-8-inch baking pan for 15 to 20 minutes. Serves 4.

 Endive is not commonly grown in the United States because of its reputation for bitterness. The more hard frosts the plant experiences, the sweeter the flavor becomes, provided, of course, that you grow a good winter-hardy strain. The English and Dutch have developed varieties better able to withstand the rain and cold, but a floating row cover or plastic cloche is recommended. Sow the seed in July or August in well-prepared soil and harvest all winter.

Herb-Stuffed Tomatoes

THIS IS A DISH for your prize winning–sized tomatoes!

6 large, firm tomatoes
4 tablespoons minced fresh basil
1 cup minced fresh parsley
2 green onions, chopped
3 cloves garlic, minced
1 teaspoon minced fresh thyme
salt to taste
freshly ground pepper to taste
¾ cup dry bread crumbs or
   Herbed Bread Crumbs (page 164)
1 tablespoon olive oil
lemon wedges, for garnish

Preheat oven to 350° F. Trim the stem end of the tomatoes. Scoop out the pulp and place in a sieve over a bowl to drain the juice. (Save the juice for another use.) Combine the pulp with the basil, parsley, green onions, garlic, and thyme. Season with salt and pepper and add the bread crumbs. Moisten the mixture with the olive oil and spoon into the tomato shells. Bake in a greased, covered casserole for 15 minutes, then uncover and bake at 400° F for 5 minutes to firm and brown the tomatoes. Serve hot with lemon wedges.
Serves 6.

Champion, Heavyweight, Beefsteak, and Large are just a few of the tomato varieties grown for "bragging" purposes. Most of the larger-fruited plants require a longer growing period and warmer evenings to ripen than our cool marine summers provide. Protection from cold and wet weather on both ends of the season will help ripen tomatoes.

Stuffed Swiss Chard Leaves

HAVE YOU EVER RETURNED home from a long hot day at your garden and discovered that your chard leaves have wilted? Take advantage of the situation with this recipe, which is easier to prepare with flexible leaves. To vary the recipe, try substituting kasha for rice, golden raisins for the regular kind, and dill seed for the dill weed.

16 Swiss chard leaves
½ cup chopped green onions
2½ cups cooked brown rice
1 cup feta cheese
½ cup cottage cheese
1 egg, beaten
½ cup chopped fresh parsley

¾ cup raisins
1 teaspoon chopped fresh dill
¼ teaspoon grated lemon zest
salt to taste
¼ teaspoon freshly ground
  pepper
2 tablespoons oil

Preheat oven to 350° F. Remove the ribs from the chard leaves and set aside. In a medium bowl, mix together the green onions, rice, feta, cottage cheese, egg, parsley, raisins, dill, lemon zest, salt, and pepper. Lay the chard leaves with the underside up and place 2 tablespoons of the filling on each leaf, one-third of the way up from the bottom. Fold over the sides of the leaf and roll up into a "square" packet. Place seam side down in a greased casserole dish. Do the same for all the leaves and brush lightly with oil. Cover and bake for about 30 minutes, or steam in a steamer basket over boiling water until the leaves are tender, about 20 minutes. Bake any extra filling and serve with the stuffed leaves.
Serves 4 to 6.

Chard is divided into two types: the thick-stemmed Swiss chard and the thin-stemmed perpetual spinach, which is really a beet. Swiss chard is the more popular type and has large leaves ideal for stuffing. One of chard's greatest virtues is that it stands up to summer heat without bolting to seed. Harvest the leaves from the outside first, working your way toward the center where the new leaves are produced. Protect them from leaf miners in the Northwest with a floating row cover.

THE CITY GARDENER'S COOKBOOK

Twice-Baked Garden Potatoes

THESE ATTRACTIVE POTATOES *come from the oven bursting with color and flavor. The recipe refers to baking potatoes, which have a thick skin and a loose internal texture and are able to hold their shape. Try serving them topped with additional cheese, yogurt, or fresh homemade salsa.*

4 large baking potatoes
1 cup fresh corn kernels
¼ cup minced red bell pepper
1 cup grated Cheddar cheese
1 tablespoon minced fresh chives
2 cloves garlic, minced
salt to taste
freshly ground pepper to taste

Preheat oven to 400° F and bake the potatoes until done, about 1 hour. Set aside to cool slightly. In a bowl, mix the corn, red pepper, cheese, chives, and garlic. Cut a slice off the top of each potato and discard. Scoop out the pulp and combine with the vegetable and cheese mixture. Season with salt and pepper. Generously fill the potatoes with the mixture. Return to the hot oven and bake for about 10 minutes or until heated through.
Serves 4.

 To many people, the thick-skinned russet potatoes are almost synonymous with baking potatoes, but of course, all potatoes can be baked. The "bakers" are a good choice for winter storage because of their sturdy skin. Before you are ready to harvest, the vines should be properly forced into dormancy, or "killed down," to help harden the tuber's skin. If you only hold back on the plant's water the tuber's size will decrease, so it is better to cut off the plant's tops and allow about two weeks for the skin to set or harden while still in the soil. Removing the foliage also keeps any diseases that the plant may have had from contaminating the tubers.

Parsnip Stuffing

PARSNIPS AND MACE OFFER *a sweet change from traditional bread and sage dressing. Plump onions and small winter squash, such as Sweet Dumpling, become little treasure chests filled with your garden bounty.*

    3 cups peeled, grated parsnips
    ½ cup chopped celery stalks and leaves
    1 cup chopped onions
    2 tablespoons oil
    ½ cup Vegetable Broth (page 26)
    3 cups cubed day-old bread
    ½ teaspoon ground cardamom
    ⅛ teaspoon ground mace
    ⅛ teaspoon freshly ground pepper
    salt to taste

In a skillet, quickly sauté the parsnips, celery, and onions in the oil. To keep from sticking, use some of the broth. Add the bread, cardamom, mace, pepper, and salt and the remaining broth and mix thoroughly. If serving as a side dish, cover and continue cooking on low heat until desired consistency is reached. Otherwise, fill your vegetables and bake until the vegetable shell is tender.
Makes 6 cups.

Celery is a cooking staple in many recipes, but as a crop it is usuall reserved for advanced or detail-oriented gardeners. It requires very rich soil, exacting temperature, copious watering, and blanching to create the tender-crisp, light stalks to which we've become accustomed. If you want to try growing celery, you can purchase from a nursery transplants that have been protected from cold night temperatures. Nights should be 50 degrees Fahrenheit before setting out the transplants.

Pastas, Savories, and Vegetable Pies

When I walk into my garden from the noisy, smelly street, within seconds
I'm transported to the countryside. The air becomes light and
fragrant, fresh and pure. I fill my lungs and kneel in the soft, yielding soil
and dig in. The smell of the soil, the flowers, the vegetables—it's a world
within a world. It takes me back to my youth when the air was cleaner
everywhere. It's the best escape therapy I know.

—A University District gardener

Garden Pasta

PASTA FRESH from your garden . . . well, almost. Tomatoes, spinach, and beets can all be cooked, pureed, and added to a base of semolina flour and eggs. Fresh herbs only need to be chopped before being kneaded in. Rich-hued vegetables impart lovely rainbow colors: ripe red tomatoes turn the dough a warm orange color; spinach produces an earthy green shade; beets result in a rosy pink pasta; and herbs become specks of green in a golden dough.

2½ **cups flour, semolina preferred**
¼ **teaspoon salt**
3 **eggs, lightly beaten**
¼ **cup vegetable puree, 2 tablespoons finely**
    chopped herbs, or 1 tablespoon pressed garlic
olive oil to moisten

In a bowl, combine the flour and salt. Form a well in the center and pour in the eggs. Gradually incorporate the flour into the eggs (your hands work best). Add the vegetable puree or herbs and knead until the dough becomes elastic. Add a little oil if the dough is stiff or a little flour if it is too sticky. The more the dough is kneaded, the better its texture, so knead at least 5 minutes. Allow the dough to rest, covered, for 1 hour to make it easier to roll out thinly, either by hand or with a pasta machine. Form into desired shapes such as ravioli or tortellini. Use the entire sheet for a poached roll, or cut into noodles such as lasagna or fettuccini. Use immediately or keep refrigerated in an airtight container. For longer storage, air dry the pasta completely, wrap tightly, and put in a cool dry place.

Spinach Lasagna: In a lasagna or sheet cake pan, layer cooked spinach noodles alternately with homemade tomato sauce, fresh basil and oregano, chopped steamed spinach, ricotta cheese, and grated mozzarella cheese, ending with a layer of mozzarella. Bake for 45 minutes to 1 hour at 350° F.
Serves 8 to 10.

Poached Pasta Roll: Lay a 12-by-12-inch thinly rolled sheet of herb pasta onto a lightweight cloth, then spread a ½-inch layer of a mixture of chopped steamed spinach, eggs, and ricotta cheese. Roll up like a jelly roll, wrap the cloth tightly, and tie the ends. Lower into a fish poacher of boiling water until submerged and poach for 40 minutes. Lift out of the water, unwrap, and transfer to a warmed serving platter. Slice and serve immediately, topped with a rich tomato, cheese, or pesto sauce.
Serves 6.

Stir-Fry and Pasta: In a wok, quickly stir-fry your favorite sliced vegetables in hot toasted sesame oil. Toss the vegetables into a bowl of hot garlic-beet noodles. Add a splash of soy sauce or other favorite seasoning and a sprinkle of sesame seeds.

Tomato Ravioli: Roll and cut tomato pasta into 2-inch squares. Put 1 teaspoon of a cheese and herb mixture in the middle of one square, moisten the edges with water, cover with another square, and press the edges to form ravioli packets. Boil for about 7 minutes, drain, and transfer to a warmed serving platter. Top with a sauce of your choice or a simple coating of sautéed garlic in olive oil.
Serves 4 to 6.

Spinach Dumplings

Dumplings tinted with garden spinach are swathed in a velvety cheese sauce touched with nutmeg.

DUMPLINGS
2 cups ricotta cheese

1 1/4 cups chopped, cooked spinach

1/2 cup freshly grated Parmesan cheese

1 egg

1 clove garlic, minced

2 tablespoons finely chopped fresh parsley

3/4 cup flour

1/2 teaspoon salt

CHEESE SAUCE
2 tablespoons butter

2 tablespoons flour

1/8 teaspoon salt

1/4 teaspoon freshly grated nutmeg

2 cups milk

1/2 cup shredded Swiss cheese

Thoroughly combine the ricotta, spinach, Parmesan, egg, garlic, and parsley. Stir in the flour and salt to make a dough (adding up to 1/4 cup more flour if needed). On a floured surface or on floured wax paper, roll and shape the dough into 1-inch balls. In a large kettle, bring about 2 to 3 quarts of water to a boil. Drop as many of the dough balls as can loosely fit in the water, cover, and simmer for 10 minutes. Lift out the dumplings with a slotted spoon, drain, and set aside, covered in a warm oven.

To make the sauce, melt the butter in a saucepan, stir in the flour, and cook until browned. Remove from the heat and add the salt, nutmeg, and milk, blending well. Return to the heat and stir constantly until thick. Add the Swiss cheese and mix until blended. Set aside. Preheat oven to broil. Spoon some of the sauce into a 9-by-13-inch baking dish, arrange the cooked dumplings, and cover them with the remaining sauce. Place the pan about 7 to 9 inches under the broiler and cook a few minutes, until warm and browned.
Serves 6.

Sweet Corn Cakes

IF ALL YOUR CORN *matures at once, you'll welcome these substantial sweet-corn pancakes to your repertoire of recipes. For a delicious breakfast serve them with butter and maple syrup (omit the pepper for breakfast cakes). For a southwestern meal, add minced hot pepper, a dollop of sour cream, and salsa.*

> **2 cups fresh corn**
> **3 eggs, beaten**
> **2 tablespoons milk**
> **1 tablespoon butter, melted**
> **1 teaspoon baking powder**
> **½ teaspoon salt**
> **⅛ teaspoon freshly ground pepper**
> **1 to 1¼ cups flour**
> **oil for frying**

In a large bowl, mix the corn, eggs, milk, and butter together. Set aside. In a separate bowl, thoroughly combine the baking powder, salt, pepper, and 1 cup of the flour. Stir the dry ingredients into the corn mixture. If necessary, add just enough additional flour to hold the fritters together. On a griddle, heat a little oil. Drop ½ cup batter onto the pan, flatten, and shape into a 5-inch cake. Cook for 3 to 5 minutes on each side, until browned. Repeat with the remainder of the batter. Serve warm with your favorite condiments. Makes eight 5-inch pancakes.

Growing sweet corn in areas with short summers is a challenge for gardeners. For best results, choose varieties that mature early, within 60 to 75 days. Most reliable in the maritime Northwest are hybrids such as Seneca Horizon, Seneca Dawn, Reward, D'Artagnan, Sugar Buns, Sweet Treat, and Spring Crystal. Corn comes in yellow, bicolor, and white varieties, so read the package information carefully. Sow seed when the soil has warmed and protect with a floating row cover until the weather has settled.

Kale Quesadillas

TRY A NORTHWEST-GROWN VERSION *of an old Mexican favorite. This festive dish is a fun new way to use your kale all year long.*

2 cups coarsely chopped kale
½ cup chopped red onions
1 tablespoon olive oil, divided
2 cloves garlic, minced
½ teaspoon ground cumin
¼ teaspoon chili powder
2 jalapeño peppers, minced
6 cherry tomatoes, halved
2 tablespoons minced fresh cilantro
6 flour tortillas
½ cup grated mozzarella cheese
salsa, yogurt, avocado slices, and
   chopped cilantro, for garnish

Steam the kale until just tender and set aside. In a skillet, sauté the onions in 1 teaspoon of the oil, until translucent. Add the garlic, cumin, and chili powder and cook an additional minute. Mix in the kale, peppers, tomatoes, and cilantro. Sauté 3 to 4 minutes, then set aside in a bowl. Wipe out the pan and add the remaining oil. Heat in preparation for browning the quesadillas. To assemble, lay out the tortillas. Place equal amounts of the kale mixture in the center of each tortilla. Sprinkle with the grated cheese. Fold them in half or shut in a square. Brown two quesadillas at a time, 2 to 3 minutes per side. Brush the pan with more oil if needed. Continue browning the others, keeping the finished ones warm in the oven. Serve topped with your homemade salsa, yogurt, avocado, and more cilantro.
Makes 6 quesadillas.

Zucchini Frittata with Basil

A FRITTATA is an Italian omelet with the filling mixed in before the eggs are cooked. Fresh baby zucchini and basil flavor this summer delicacy. Try adding diced red pepper and replacing half of the zucchini with yellow summer squash for color.

    1 medium onion, chopped
    4 cloves garlic, sliced
    2 tablespoons olive oil
    8 baby zucchini, sliced
    ½ cup chopped fresh basil or ¼ cup Basil Pesto (page 142)
    6 large eggs
    salt to taste
    freshly ground pepper to taste

In a large skillet with a tight-fitting lid, place the onion and garlic in the oil. Sauté over medium heat until the onion is transparent. Add the zucchini and basil or pesto and cook, stirring occasionally, about 3 to 5 minutes, until the squash is just tender. In a bowl, lightly beat the eggs and add the salt and pepper. Pour the eggs into the squash mixture and stir briefly. The eggs should just cover the vegetables. Cover and cook until the eggs are just set, about 5 minutes. Pour off any excess liquid. Loosen the frittata from the side of the pan and unmold onto a platter. Serve hot or cold.
Serves 4.

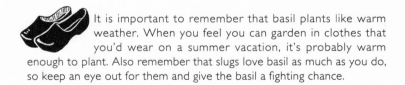 It is important to remember that basil plants like warm weather. When you feel you can garden in clothes that you'd wear on a summer vacation, it's probably warm enough to plant. Also remember that slugs love basil as much as you do, so keep an eye out for them and give the basil a fighting chance.

Tomatillo Pizza

HERE'S A CREATIVE *and easy way to use some of your tomatillo sauce and lots of cherry tomatoes. These are thin-crust pizzas, especially good for appetizers, but you can also make thick-pizza crust and turn this combination of cheeses, tomatoes, and peppers into a main meal. Late summer rains can cause Sweet 100s and other cherry tomatoes to crack; then suddenly, you have too many to eat all at once. Rather than let them go to waste, pop them into a freezer bag as fast as they ripen, and you'll have an excellent reserve of tomatoes all year long.*

> 1 12-inch whole wheat chapati or tortilla
> ½ cup Tomatillo Sauce (page 137)
> ½ cup grated mozzarella cheese
> ½ cup grated jalapeño jack cheese
> ½ bell pepper, green, red, yellow, chocolate,
>   or a mixture, sliced
> 2 green onions, chopped
> ¼ cup chopped black olives
> 10 Sweet 100s cherry tomatoes, halved

Preheat oven to 400° F. Put the chapati or tortilla on a pizza pan and allow it to crisp in the oven. When crisp, spread with the tomatillo sauce, then layer with the cheeses, pepper, onions, olives, and tomatoes. Bake until bubbly and brown, about 5 minutes. Makes one 12-inch pizza.

Besides causing tomatoes to split, late summer or early fall rains create the ideal environment for late blight to blacken and rot your tomato plants. (Do not compost affected plants.) Protect your harvest from heavy rains by providing a plastic cover or umbrella at the end of the season.

Zucchini Pizzas

THE LARGE, PRICKLY, TROPICAL LEAVES *of the zucchini plant cast protective shadows over its nest of treasures. Inevitably this shadow hides one zucchini that grows beyond its prime. But giant zucchini are the perfect base for these no-crust vegetarian "pizzas," provided they haven't started forming hard seeds. These pizzas are a fun treat for kids, and they take so little time to prepare that you can stay and enjoy the beauty of the shadow patterns in your garden a while longer.*

    8 zucchini slices, ³⁄₄ inch thick, 4 inches in diameter
    salt to taste
    freshly ground pepper to taste
    2 teaspoons chopped fresh basil
    2 teaspoons chopped fresh oregano
    ¹⁄₂ cup chopped fresh parsley
    8 tomato slices, ¹⁄₄ inch thick
    8 onion slices, ¹⁄₄ inch thick
    8 slices of mozzarella, provolone, Monterey jack,
        or other cheese

Preheat oven to 325° F. Place the zucchini slices on a greased baking pan. Sprinkle with the salt, pepper, basil, oregano, and parsley. Lay a slice of tomato on top of the seasonings, followed by the onion and topped by the cheese. Bake for about 10 minutes, until the cheese turns bubbly.
Serves 4.

An organic method for keeping mildew off a squash plant's leaves and stems in those last humid days of summer seemed impossible until experiments with common baking soda showed positive results. Many gardeners have had their own recipes for years, and recently garden magazines have been excitedly reporting "new" findings. Here's a recipe that might work for your mildew problems: Dissolve 1 tablespoon of baking soda in a gallon of water and add 2 ½ tablespoons of horticultural oil to act as a spreading agent. Spray weekly on the top and bottom of the squash leaves before mildew begins.

Kohlrabi Pie

THIS IS A TAKE-OFF on a Russian cabbage pie, using another member of the diverse cole family, the kohlrabi. If you don't grow kohlrabi, you can substitute grated cabbage. The addition of an egg keeps the pie crust flaky and prevents it from shrinking during baking.

PIE CRUST

    1 ¼ cups chilled pastry flour

    ½ cup chilled butter

    1 egg, lightly beaten

    1 tablespoon finely minced herbs, ground nuts, or seeds

    3 to 4 tablespoons cold water

Sift the flour to aerate it. In a medium bowl, cut the butter into the flour until the texture is the consistency of cornmeal. Add the egg and the herbs, nuts, or seeds, then gradually add the water, 1 tablespoon at a time. Lightly work the dough just until it forms a ball; the dough will become tough if overworked. Chill, covered, for several hours or quickly roll the dough on a floured board. Shape the pastry into the pan; trim and shape the edges. Keep the dough as cool as possible until ready to bake.
Makes one 9-inch crust.

FILLING

    3 cups peeled, grated kohlrabi

    2 tablespoons olive oil, divided

    2 tablespoons minced fresh dill

    ½ cup sliced mushrooms

    1 cup sliced onions

    2 teaspoons minced fresh tarragon

    2 tablespoons minced fresh basil

    2 eggs, lightly beaten

    1 cup cottage cheese

    ¼ cup freshly grated Parmesan cheese

Preheat oven to 350° F. Prick the pie crust with a fork, line with foil and weight with uncooked rice or beans. Bake for 15 minutes, then remove foil and beans.

In a large skillet, sauté the kohlrabi in 1 tablespoon of the oil for 5 to 10 minutes. Add the dill and set aside in a bowl. Sauté the mushrooms and onions in the remaining tablespoon of oil until the liquid given off by the mushrooms evaporates. Add the tarragon and basil, remove from the heat, and set aside. In a small bowl, combine the eggs, cottage cheese, and half of the Parmesan. Spread the kohlrabi in the pie crust. Top with the mushrooms and onions, followed by the cheese and egg mixture. Sprinkle with the remaining Parmesan and bake for 30 minutes, or until golden brown. Serves 6.

During one fall P-Patch work party, an abandoned kohlrabi the size of a honeydew melon was discovered among the weeds. Amazingly, it was still crisp and flavorful throughout. The huge root was divided up and eaten fresh with dips, in soups, and in this pie, too. Unfortunately, the gardener's growing secrets for such a legendary kohlrabi were never revealed. We can, however, offer this advice: as with other cole crops, start with a rich soil, add lime, cover with a floating row cover, and keep well-watered. You may grow a spectacular kohlrabi, too.

Couscous Cauliflower Pie

IF YOU'VE NEVER TRIED couscous, here's your chance. This tiny member of the pasta family is popular in African and Middle Eastern cultures. Its short cooking time lets you tend your crops a little longer. The fragrance given off by the feathery, fragrant leaves of fresh dill can be enjoyed during harvest as well as at the table. Try dressing up this vegetable pie with Tomatoes Intensified (page 150); they add marvelous flavor and a vivid color contrast to the white cauliflower and golden couscous.

1 tablespoon olive oil
1 cup uncooked couscous
1½ cups boiling water
3 tablespoons butter
½ cup diced onions
2 cloves garlic, crushed
⅔ cup grated carrots
2 cups chopped cauliflower
2 tablespoons chopped
   fresh dill

⅛ teaspoon freshly grated
   nutmeg
1 tablespoon soy sauce
   or tamari
freshly ground pepper to taste
3 eggs, lightly beaten
1½ cups grated Cheddar
   cheese
½ cup sour cream

Preheat oven to 350° F. In a small saucepan, heat the olive oil and add the couscous. Stir over medium heat for about 3 minutes and pour in the boiling water, then remove from heat. Cover tightly and let stand 20 minutes, or until all of the water is absorbed. In a skillet, melt the butter and add the onions, garlic, carrots, and cauliflower. Sauté the vegetables until just tender. Remove from heat and mix them with the couscous in a large bowl. Stir in the dill, nutmeg, soy sauce or tamari, pepper, eggs, cheese, and sour cream. Spread the mixture evenly in a 10-inch pie pan. Bake, covered, for 35 minutes. Remove cover and bake another 10 minutes, until the top is slightly brown. Cool for 10 minutes before cutting into wedges.
Serves 6.

French Sorrel–Onion Tart

THE TANGY TASTE OF SORREL harmonizes with smoky Gruyère in this rich and elegant tart. Sorrel is a striking accent in a fresh salad but is most often used to flavor cooked vegetable dishes. To avoid discoloration, chop sorrel only with a stainless steel knife and never cook it in an iron pan. Calorie watchers may substitute low-fat milk for the cream in this recipe.

1 9-inch single pie crust,
    prebaked (see recipe under
    Kohlrabi Pie, page 124)
3 tablespoons butter
1 large red onion, thinly sliced
4 cups stemmed and sliced
    French sorrel leaves
2 large eggs

1 cup cream
¼ cup grated Gruyère
    cheese
pinch of freshly grated
    nutmeg
salt to taste
freshly ground pepper
    to taste

Preheat oven to 375° F. To prebake pie crust, prick the bottom and sides with a fork. Line the crust with foil and weight with uncooked rice or beans. Bake for 10 to 20 minutes. Remove foil and beans.

In a skillet, melt the butter and add the onion. Cook for about 5 minutes, or until the onion is soft. Add the sorrel and continue cooking over low heat. When the sorrel is wilted, remove from heat and set aside. In a medium bowl, whisk the eggs and cream. Add half of the Gruyère cheese and the onion and sorrel. Mix together before seasoning with the nutmeg, salt, and pepper. Layer the other half of the grated cheese over the crust and pour the filling on top. Bake for 35 minutes, until set.
Serves 6.

French sorrel is an easy-to-grow, all-season, hardy, 2-foot perennial green with a tart flavor. Keep these shade-tolerant plants well watered and the flower stocks cut back for a continuous reward of lush, tender leaves. One plant is generally sufficient for a family.

Red Tomato Tart

VINE-RIPENED TOMATOES from your garden are marinated lightly, laid atop a crisp almond crust, and sprinkled with cheeses. The tart is then quickly broiled for a summery Italian treat. Try different colored varieties of tomatoes such as yellow, pink, orange, or even white.

PASTRY

1 ½ cups flour
½ cup finely ground almonds
⅛ teaspoon salt
⅓ cup butter
2 tablespoons cold water
⅓ cup oil

TOPPING

6 to 8 medium tomatoes, sliced ½ inch thick
½ cup extra virgin olive oil
3 cloves garlic, minced
¼ cup chopped fresh parsley
2 tablespoons chopped fresh basil
2 tablespoons chopped fresh lemon thyme
freshly ground pepper to taste
½ cup chopped red onions
1 tablespoon butter
4 large mushrooms, chopped
2 tablespoons Dijon mustard
¼ cup freshly grated Parmesan cheese
4 tablespoons finely grated Monterey jack cheese

Preheat oven to 450° F. To make the pastry, combine the flour, almonds, and salt in a bowl. Cut in the butter until evenly textured. Add the water and oil, blending lightly. Press the pastry into a 12-inch pizza pan, shape an edge, and prick evenly with a fork to avoid steam pockets. Bake for 10 minutes, then reduce heat to 350° F and bake an additional 15 minutes or until golden brown.

Lay the tomato slices in a single layer in a shallow pan and set aside. In a small bowl, combine the oil, garlic, parsley, basil, lemon thyme, and pepper. Pour the mixture over the tomatoes and marinate at room temperature for 1 hour.

In a skillet, sauté the onions in butter until tender. Add the mushrooms, cook for 1 minute, and set aside. Spread the mustard on the baked crust, followed by the onion-mushroom mixture. Sprinkle with Parmesan. Drain the marinated tomatoes, being careful to save the herbs. (The extra marinade makes an excellent salad dressing.) Sprinkle the jack cheese over the tomatoes to create a lacy covering. Put in a warm oven or quickly broil until the cheese is just melted. Serve at room temperature.
Serves 4 to 6.

Rotation of crops is one of the easiest ways to keep your plants disease free. Many pests favor a particular family of plants; keeping them rotated will slow the pest build-up in your garden. Potatoes, tomatoes, and eggplant as well as peppers, tomatillos, and even ground cherries are all closely related; therefore, be sure to plant them where no family member was planted the previous year.

Spring Greens Pie

THIS DISH IS SIMILAR TO CLASSIC Greek spinach pie, but it allows you to be as versatile as your garden is unique. The puff pastry (found in the frozen food section) makes this an impressive dish to serve at special occasions. The filling can be made ahead of time and the pie put together at the last minute. For a change, add a handful of purslane, amaranth, watercress or upland cress, or even radish tops.

1 cup sliced carrots	½ cup freshly grated
10 cups chopped assorted	Parmesan cheese or
greens, spinach, New Zealand	crumbled feta cheese
spinach, arugula, kale, or	1 egg
beet greens	1 teaspoon cinnamon
1½ cups cottage cheese	1 teaspoon celery seeds

Fill the bottom of a Dutch oven with the carrots and as many greens as will fit. Cook over medium heat, relying on the water left on the washed greens to cook the carrots. When the first batch of greens wilts, stir in the rest and cook until the carrots are tender, about 5 to 8 minutes. Cool and squeeze the excess liquid from the greens and set aside. In a medium-sized mixing bowl, mix the cheeses, spices and egg. Add the mushrooms and leeks or green onions. Combine with the greens and carrots.

Preheat oven to 375° F while the puff pastry is thawing. In a 9-by-13-inch pan, sprinkle the couscous and distribute evenly. Carefully distribute the filling over the couscous. When the pastry is just thawed, open and roll two-thirds of it to the length of the pan. Use the other third to fill edges or cut to make a decorative topping. Bake for 40 to 45 minutes, until the pastry is puffy in the middle.
Serves 6.

Valentine Beet Quiche

HERE IS A HEARTY, VIBRANT *version of the routine quiche. A flaky pie crust is filled with a custardlike cheese and egg base interlaced with an out-of-the-ordinary vegetable. Use red beets and a heart-shaped cake pan to make a memorable quiche for Valentine's Day. But you don't have to wait until February; you can harvest beets year-round. Use golden beets for a harvest moon pie, or try white beets, which result in a quiche almost as sweet as a dessert. Add caraway or dill seeds to the pie crust for a unique touch.*

> 1 9-inch single pie crust, prebaked (see recipe under
>   Kohlrabi Pie, page 124)
> 2 cups cooked, peeled, and grated beets
> 1 cup milk or cream
> 2 large eggs, lightly beaten
> 1 cup freshly grated Parmesan cheese, divided
> freshly ground pepper to taste

Preheat oven to 375° F. To prebake the pie crust, prick the bottom and sides with a fork. Line the pie crust with foil and weight with uncooked rice or beans. Bake for 10 minutes, until lightly cooked. Remove foil and beans. Lower the temperature to 350° F.

In a small bowl, mix the beets, milk or cream, and eggs together. Stir in one third of the cheese and pour into the pie crust. Sprinkle the remaining cheese on top and bake for 25 to 30 minutes, until golden brown and center is set. Cool slightly before cutting.
Serves 6 to 8.

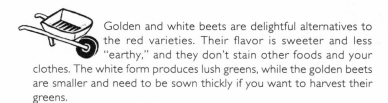

Golden and white beets are delightful alternatives to the red varieties. Their flavor is sweeter and less "earthy," and they don't stain other foods and your clothes. The white form produces lush greens, while the golden beets are smaller and need to be sown thickly if you want to harvest their greens.

Winter Onion Pie
with Fresh Nutmeg

SERVED HOT, WARM, OR COLD, *this savory pie is comfort food. The long, slow precooking of the onions brings out their sweetness.*

1 9-inch single pie crust, prebaked
  (see recipe under Kohlrabi Pie, page 124)
3 cups chopped yellow onions
1 tablespoon olive oil
1 tablespoon flour
2 eggs, beaten
½ cup milk
1 teaspoon salt
⅛ teaspoon freshly ground pepper
⅛ teaspoon freshly grated nutmeg

Preheat oven to 375° F. To prebake the pie crust, prick the bottom and sides with a fork. Line the crust with foil and weight with uncooked rice or beans. Bake 10 to 20 minutes. Remove foil and beans.

In a skillet, cook the onions and oil together very slowly over low heat for 1 hour, stirring occasionally. Sprinkle in the flour, stir, and cook a few minutes until thickened. Remove from heat and set aside. In a large bowl, combine the eggs, milk, salt, pepper, and nutmeg. Add the cooked onions to the egg mixture and stir gently. Fill the prebaked pie crust and bake for 30 minutes, until golden. Serves 6 to 8.

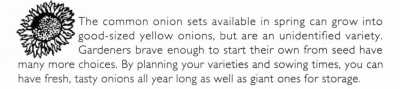 The common onion sets available in spring can grow into good-sized yellow onions, but are an unidentified variety. Gardeners brave enough to start their own from seed have many more choices. By planning your varieties and sowing times, you can have fresh, tasty onions all year long as well as giant ones for storage.

Sauces

*I will always have in my memory the time I went out to the garden early
on a Sunday morning after a light rain. The breeze was blowing
ever so slightly, and I could smell the spicy basil and
oregano we had planted. I can smell it now!*

—A Jackson Park gardener

Fresh Summer Tomato Sauce

JUICY RED TOMATOES STILL WARM *from the sun are combined with sprigs of just-picked oregano and basil in this easy, light pasta sauce. The only cooking required is the natural kind under the glorious blue skies of summer. This sauce is exceptionally good over tortellini.*

2½ cups chopped tomatoes
¾ cup chopped green bell peppers
1 clove garlic, minced
½ cup olive oil
3 teaspoons chopped fresh oregano
1 tablespoon chopped fresh basil

In a bowl, mix all the ingredients and let stand for at least 10 minutes. Serve the sauce over hot pasta.
Makes 3 cups.

When a tomato plant has abnormal-looking leaves, how can you tell if it is suffering? Rolled leaves can be a sign of drought, but if the plant has been watered, you needn't be concerned about this. You should know, however, that tomato plants will reveal herbicide damage in their leaves. In such a case, the leaf will appear contorted, with the veins growing in a parallel pattern similar to grass, unlike the leaf of the standard dicot, with veins branching in a 90-degree pattern. It is advisable not to eat any fruit that has formed on such a plant. Do not be confused by tomato plants that have a simple potato foliage, such as the Brandy Wine or Stupice varieties.

Garlicky Tomato-Eggplant Sauce

THIS RICH TOMATO SAUCE, *brimming with an abundant array of fresh herbs, eggplant, and tomato, is saturated with enough garlic to send garlic worshipers into a state of bliss. Eggplant gives the sauce substance; cherry tomatoes lend sweetness; red wine carries the pungency of the herbs; and the garlic has the final say.*

¼ cup olive oil

10 cloves garlic, minced

¾ cup finely chopped onions

3 cups peeled, cubed eggplant

1 cup minced fresh parsley

¼ cup minced fresh oregano

1 tablespoon minced fresh basil

½ teaspoon salt

½ cup dry red wine

¼ cup water

2 cups Sweet 100s cherry
   tomatoes

freshly ground pepper
   to taste

3 tablespoons freshly grated
   Parmesan cheese

In a skillet, heat the oil and sauté the garlic and onions until lightly browned. Add the eggplant, parsley, oregano, basil, and salt. Cover and simmer for about 15 minutes. As the eggplant cooks down, add the wine and the water and continue cooking until the mixture has the consistency of a sauce. Just before serving, add the tomatoes and pepper, cooking long enough to heat thoroughly, yet retaining the tomato shape. Sprinkle with the freshly grated Parmesan. Makes about 4 cups.

If you have trouble peeling cloves of garlic, try growing the variety Rocambole. It forms rather large cloves around a central stem and has thick purplish skins that are easier to remove. In the moderate winters of the maritime Northwest, the largest cluster of cloves harvested in late summer result from planting the largest individual cloves in the fall. Rocambole is an eye-catching plant because of its curly, pig's tail–like flower stem that produces a cluster of tiny garlic cloves.

Thai Peanut Sauce

THIS SAUCE TAKES ON AN ETHNIC flavor as peanut butter shares the billing with freshly grated ginger, soy sauce, and a touch of honey. Dark and thick, it is delectable when poured over a bed of lightly steamed green vegetables such as spinach, kale, chard, collards, bok choy, or Chinese broccoli. In fact, this sauce is good with any combination of vegetables and is especially dazzling when accented with roasted red pepper strips and white cubes of firm tofu.

1 cup chopped onions
2 cloves garlic, minced
2 tablespoons grated fresh ginger
3 tablespoons oil
1 jalapeño pepper, finely chopped
1 cup peanut butter
1½ cups water
¼ cup soy sauce or tamari
2 tablespoons honey
cilantro or Holy basil, for garnish

In a skillet, sauté the onions, garlic, and ginger in hot oil until tender. Add the jalepeño pepper, peanut butter, water, soy sauce or tamari, and honey and mix thoroughly. Slowly cook the sauce until it thickens. Serve with cilantro or basil as garnish.
Makes 4 cups.

Exotic foreign flavors come from herbs and spices such as ginger, chilies, and Holy basil. The tropical perennial ginger root is challenging to grow without a hot house. Some of the annual crops, like cilantro and Holy basil, will grow in a sunny Northwest garden. Holy basil, a fuzzy-leafed tender perennial, can be started from seed or planted from starts when the weather settles. Provide the same conditions as with other basil and pinch the growth tips to induce bushiness. Harvest leaves and sprigs before they flower for the best flavor. Pots of Holy basil can be brought inside for winter use.

Tomatillo Sauce

"TOMATILLO" MEANS "LITTLE TOMATO" in Spanish. What makes tomatillos so interesting is their "packaging"; when ready to be picked, they fill the papery brown covering. A well-grown tomatillo plant produces enough fruit to double or triple this recipe easily. This versatile sauce can be enjoyed as a topping on a homemade pizza crust, as a dip with your favorite chips, or in a corn tortilla filled with cheese, olives, and sour cream.

  12 medium tomatillos, husked
  1 jalepeño pepper, stemmed and seeded
  3 tablespoons minced fresh cilantro
  ½ cup chopped onions
  1 clove garlic
  1 teaspoon oil
  2 cups chicken broth

In a food processor, combine the tomatillos, jalepeño pepper, cilantro, onions, and garlic into a smooth mixture. Set aside. In a large skillet, heat the oil, then cook the tomatillo puree until thick and dark in color, about 10 minutes. Stir occasionally. Add the broth and simmer until reduced to a thick sauce, about 30 minutes. Makes 4 to 5 cups.

 As exotic as tomatillos might seem to most of us, the plants actually grow quite well in the Pacific Northwest, sometimes even better than many tomatoes. Since they can reseed in the garden if even one fruit is left to overwinter, it's a good idea always to clean up disease-harboring plant material in the fall. Leftover seeds will grow into productive plants next spring without the bother of transplants and cloches. Gardeners have sustained hundreds of unusual strains of tomatillos over the years, offering many of them to the Seed Savers Association.

Fragrant Cilantro Sauce

FRESH-SCENTED CILANTRO DOMINATES *this culinary delight.*
The testers who prepared the recipe competed in their praise of this
"absolutely heavenly" sauce. When cilantro is abundant in your
garden, prepare extra batches of the sauce; it can be frozen for several
months. This aromatic sauce is especially good on freshly cooked corn
on the cob, slices of juicy tomatoes, or crisp, nutty crackers.

> 2 cups chopped fresh cilantro
> ½ cup chopped fresh parsley
> ½ cup chopped scallions or green onions
> ½ cup walnuts
> 2 cloves garlic
> 6 cooked prunes, chopped, or ¼ cup stewed raisins
> ¼ cup fresh lemon juice
> 1 cup walnut oil
> salt to taste
> freshly ground pepper to taste

In a food processor, combine the cilantro, parsley, scallions or
green onions, walnuts, garlic, and prunes or raisins. Mix thoroughly
before adding the lemon juice, oil, salt, and pepper.
Makes 4 cups.

Scallions, sometimes mistakenly called green onions, are
actually multiplier onions known by different names, such as
Welch onion, Nebuka, Chang Fa, or bunching onions. They
can only be started from seed and will grow into a clump of
long straight onions, unlike green onions, which are started from either
seed or a set but eventually form a bulb. Use a high-nitrogen organic
fertilizer and expect a beautiful plant that can reach 4 feet in height but
more commonly grows to 2 feet. Available for harvest all year long, the
plants reseed themselves, so you only have to plant once. A small
space is all that's required.

Rhubarb-Orange Sauce with Ginger

LIVELY, PIQUANT, AND NOT TOO SWEET, *this sauce is delightful served over ice cream, with gingerbread, or beside a main dish.*

3 cups chopped fresh rhubarb
⅓ cup sugar
½ cup fresh orange juice
3 tablespoons grated orange zest
2-inch piece ginger, pressed and pulp discarded

In a heavy saucepan, combine the rhubarb, sugar, orange juice, orange zest, and ginger juice. Heat to boiling. Reduce heat and simmer, uncovered, for about 30 minutes or until thick. Remove from heat and cool to room temperature.
Makes 1½ to 2 cups.

 Rhubarb plants love to be fed lots of nutrients, so add a bag of composted manure as a top dressing for the plants in the spring each year. For best stem production, cut out any flower stalks when they form; the tall, creamy white flowers, though pretty, will form seed and diminish the size of the plant. Remember that the leaves are poisonous.

Carrot and Yam Sauce

THIS WARM ORANGE-COLORED MEDLEY of root crop vegetables
blended into a thick, smooth sauce is a good substitute for the more
traditional red pasta sauce. Whole cloves, freshly grated ginger, and
caraway seeds enhance the flavors over time. Try this as a tasty
topping on Sweet Corn Cakes (page 119).

2 cups chopped onions
2 tablespoons olive oil
2 whole cloves
1/8 teaspoon ground cumin
1/8 teaspoon celery seeds
1 teaspoon chopped fresh
   thyme leaves
1 teaspoon chopped fresh
   oregano
1 teaspoon chopped
   fresh basil

1/4 cup chopped fresh parsley
1 bay leaf
1/4 teaspoon grated fresh
   ginger
1/4 teaspoon caraway seeds
4 cups grated carrots
1 cup grated potatoes
3/4 cup chopped celery
1 cup peeled, grated yams

In a skillet, sauté the onions in the oil until tender. Add the cloves,
cumin, celery seeds, thyme, oregano, basil, parsley, bay leaf, ginger,
and caraway seeds. Stir together and cook over low heat for another minute, then set aside. In a large saucepan, place the carrots,
potatoes, celery, and yams. Add the onion mixture and enough
water to barely cover the vegetables. Bring to a boil, then reduce
heat to low and cook for 1 hour, stirring occasionally.
Makes 8 cups.

Yams grow in hot humid climates. If your growing conditions
are less than perfect, you might want to try *Dioscorea batata*, a
hardy perennial Chinese yam, which is used extensively in Asia.
This interesting plant is worth growing for its beautiful heart-shaped
leaves and flowers that smell of cinnamon; hence its alternate name,
Cinnamon Vine. The white-fleshed tubers can grow as large as 2
pounds the first year and will become larger, up to 3 feet in length the
second year if left in the ground.

Garbanzo Bean and Tomato Sauce

The firm texture and nutlike flavor of garbanzo beans harmonize well with the sharper tastes of fresh tomatoes and basil. Serve this hearty supper fare over grains such as quinoa or kasha. For a spicier version, sauté hot green or red peppers with the onions; then add fresh corn to the mixture for the last 5 minutes of cooking.

1 cup chopped onions
1 clove garlic, minced
2 tablespoons olive oil
2 cups cooked, drained garbanzo beans
2 cups chopped tomatoes
1 cup Vegetable Broth (page 26)
1 bay leaf
1 tablespoon minced fresh basil
salt to taste
freshly ground pepper to taste

In a skillet, sauté the onions and garlic in oil until tender. Add the garbanzo beans and tomatoes and mix together. Stir in the broth, bay leaf, basil, salt, and pepper. Bring to a boil, reduce the heat, and simmer for 20 minutes. Remove the bay leaf before serving. Makes 3 to 4 cups.

Although regular garbanzo beans are grown in climates hotter than the Pacific Northwest, you might want to try growing the variety Kabuli Black, released by Washington State University. They are more tolerant of cold soil and more vigorous. The plant looks like lace glistening with jewels and it changes color in the fall. The beans themselves are charcoal black and come two to a pod.

Basil Pesto

THIS IS A GOOD BASIC PESTO *that transforms delicate hand-picked sprigs of basil into a lusty, addictive sauce. Add a touch of class with a little cream in the final blending of toasted pine nuts and fresh basil. To show off your creative spirit, consider using purple basils for a pretty pink pesto.*

2 cups chopped fresh basil
3 cloves garlic
⅓ cup extra virgin olive oil
⅓ cup freshly grated Parmesan cheese
½ teaspoon salt
¼ teaspoon freshly ground pepper
¼ cup toasted pine nuts

In a food processor, combine the basil, garlic, olive oil, Parmesan, salt, and pepper and mix until smooth. Add the pine nuts and process quickly to retain some of the nuts' crunchy texture. Serve hot or cold.
Makes 1 cup.

To enjoy your favorite basil throughout the winter when fresh garden basil is unavailable, make extra batches of pesto and freeze it in ice cube trays. Pop the frozen pesto cubes into a freezer bag for easy access. Each cube is the equivalent of about 1 tablespoon of sauce.

Purple, Purple Ruffle and Opal basils are beautiful burgundy-leafed plants with unique flavors that many cooks prize. They require the same warm and sunny weather as regular green basil. Basils are attractive as ornamental plants because of their foliage and lavender-pink flowers.

Garlic Green Pesto

A GARLIC LOVER'S DELIGHT, *this beautiful emerald green spread allows you to present to your guests a garlic bread with a difference that only gardeners can provide. Garlic greens are used like chives or green onions and blend well with pine nuts, freshly grated cheeses, and oregano. Awaken those taste buds by serving lots of hot pasta smothered under a blanket of garlicky green pesto.*

1 ½ **cups chopped tender garlic greens**
½ **cup pine nuts, chopped**
¾ **cup freshly grated Parmesan, Romano, or Asiago cheese**
1 **tablespoon chopped fresh oregano**
salt to taste
freshly ground pepper to taste
½ **cup extra virgin olive oil**

In a food processor, combine the garlic greens, pine nuts, cheese, oregano, salt, and pepper. Slowly drizzle in the olive oil as you continue the blending process until the sauce reaches a smooth, thick consistency.
Makes 1 ½ cups.

Plant lots of garlic in the fall. What better way is there to utilize your winter soil? From a garlic bulb cluster, save the apparently useless, hard to peel little cloves or the tiny top bulblets that form on the "flower" stem. Plant them in a row to harvest later as garlic greens. These greens can be substituted for chives and green onion tops. The garlic that you don't use for greens will form bulbs and be ready to harvest before you need the space for a summer crop. Let the tops bend over on their own, then slow down the watering to allow the plants to become dormant. After they have turned brown, dig them up and continue the drying process in a well-ventilated area.

Herb Garden Pesto

"FRESH IS BEST" says it all when it comes to a pesto that is jam-packed with six of your favorite garden-fresh herbs. Whether you prepare a hot linguini, a crusty warm bread with melted cheese, a fresh vegetable soup, or a cool summer pasta salad, this unique pesto ensures that the results will be a culinary delight.

1 cup fresh basil
1 cup fresh parsley
2 tablespoons fresh dill
2 tablespoons fresh chives
1 tablespoon fresh oregano or marjoram
1 tablespoon fresh rosemary or thyme leaves
½ cup chopped walnuts or slivered almonds
½ cup extra virgin olive oil
⅓ cup freshly grated Parmesan cheese
1 tablespoon fresh lemon juice
1 clove garlic
¼ teaspoon freshly ground pepper

In a food processor, combine all of the ingredients and process until the pesto becomes smooth and even textured. Add more olive oil if necessary. Serve fresh on pasta, bread, or in soups. Makes 1 cup.

Each of the herbs in this recipe has a low-growing bush variety available that can be planted on the border of your vegetable and flower gardens. Seed the summer basil and dill between widely spaced plants of parsley, chives, and oregano. Planting creatively for both interest and diversity is good for your visual and culinary pleasure.

Italian Parsley Pesto

THE BEAUTY OF THIS PARSLEY PESTO *is in its lovely, intense, spring-green color. This dip is outstanding on an antipasto tray or as a starter at a multicourse meal. Deep orange baby carrots are especially attractive served with this dark green pesto. If you don't have Italian parsley in your garden, curly and Hamburg parsley are good substitutes.*

1 cup lightly packed Italian parsley leaves
½ cup freshly grated Parmesan cheese
⅓ cup extra virgin olive oil
1 clove garlic
salt to taste
freshly ground pepper to taste

In a food processor, combine the parsley, Parmesan, olive oil, and garlic. Puree until the consistency is smooth. Season with salt and pepper. If made ahead of time, cover and refrigerate up to 2 days; otherwise, serve at room temperature.
Makes 1 cup.

Beginning gardeners too often have the heartbreak of a lost carrot crop. Lots of people give up on growing carrots in the Northwest because of carrot rust fly damage to the roots. The secret is to cover the crop from seed to harvest with a floating row cover such as Reemay or Agronet.

Dill Pesto

THIS FRESH-TASTING SAUCE *is a cool-weather variation on the traditional heat-seeking ingredient of basil pesto. Unlike basil pesto, a parsley and dill pesto will retain its bright green color. No dairy products are used in this version; the dill balances the flavor without requiring any cheese. Freeze an extra batch to capture the penetrating dill flavor all year.*

> 3 cloves garlic
> 1 tablespoon grated lemon zest
> 1¾ cups chopped fresh parsley
> ⅓ cup chopped fresh dill
> juice of half a lemon
> ¼ cup extra virgin olive oil

In a food processor, combine the garlic, lemon zest, parsley, dill, and lemon juice. With the processor running, slowly pour in the oil and puree until smooth. Serve over pasta or vegetables. Makes 1½ cups.

Dill is a hardy annual that prefers a warm location protected from the wind. The green threadlike foliage, called dill weed, is hard to come by unless homegrown. Because the plant goes to seed quickly, successive sowings are necessary to have a continuous supply of greens. Allowing some of the plants to go to seed is a good idea since the seeds are a useful culinary ingredient. Dill weed does not dehydrate well; most of its flavor is lost during the drying process.

Cilantro and Pumpkin-Seed Pesto

CILANTRO FANS WILL WANT to try this unusual pesto made with pumpkin seeds. The flavor enhances potatoes as well as pasta. Roasted peanuts can be substituted for the pumpkin seeds, or add a pinch of hot peppers for a south-of-the-border pesto.

2 cups lightly packed fresh cilantro
⅓ cup hulled pumpkin seeds
½ cup freshly grated Parmesan cheese
¼ cup olive oil
5 tablespoons fresh lemon juice
5 cloves garlic, chopped
½ teaspoon salt

In a food processor, combine the cilantro and pumpkin seeds with the seasonings, pureeing until the sauce forms a smooth, even texture. Store in a jar in the refrigerator for up to 2 weeks, or freeze for winter use.
Makes 2 cups.

The distinctive flavor of the beautiful cilantro plant is usually either adored or hated; for some, it becomes an acquired taste. Before making a huge batch of something calling for the herb, decide which way your allegiance falls. If you find that the flavor isn't for you, remember that the plant, with its whitish pink wispy flowers, is still highly ornamental in any garden. Once the seeds of the cilantro plant mature, they are harvested as coriander and can be used in rice and dessert dishes.

Hot Tomatillo and Jalapeño Salsa

THIS FIERY COMBINATION *of jalapeño peppers, cilantro, and tomatillos might provide the inspiration to create a Mexican-style feast. Become more adventurous in the garden by growing tomatillos and fresh cilantro along with different hot peppers. Since the salsa freezes well, save some to warm up a cold winter day.*

10 green tomatillos
4 cloves garlic
8 medium jalapeño peppers
1 cup firmly packed cilantro
3 tablespoons fresh lime juice
2 tablespoons oil
salt to taste

Prepare the tomatillos by removing and discarding the husks and stems. In a saucepan, place them in enough water to cover and bring to a boil over medium-high heat. Cook the tomatillos until they are almost tender, about 5 minutes. Drain and rinse, then drain again and set aside. In a food processor, combine the garlic, jalapeño peppers, cilantro, lime juice, and tomatillos. Quickly puree the mixture, keeping the chunky texture. Transfer to a bowl and add the oil and salt. Whisk together and serve with your favorite chips.
Makes 2½ cups.

Jalapeño and other small-fruited hot pepper plants, usually associated with the hotter regions, grow remarkably well in cooler areas if they are given a good sunny location. Set out plants in June and protect with a floating row cover or cloche. Although not as fiery as it would be if grown in hotter regions, the fruit is abundant. The flavor can be intensified by including the inner membrane and seeds when cooking, but wear rubber gloves when chopping the peppers to avoid accidentally rubbing your eyes!

Chunky Salsa

QUICKLY PULSED IN A FOOD PROCESSOR *or hand chopped, the simple ingredients of tomatoes, jalapeños, onion, and of course, cilantro, form the quintessential version of salsa. Aside from serving salsa with chips, consider using it to top your out-of-the-garden baked potato— salsa delivers vibrant taste without the fat associated with the standard topping of sour cream. On your next lunch break, have a salsa-topped potato instead of a cold sandwich. Gardeners can use their yellow or orange tomatoes to make a unique salsa that can't fail to impress their nongardening friends. If the tomatoes used are sweet, low-acid types, the salsa might need a little more bite. Try adding a teaspoon of cider or red wine vinegar or a splash of lime.*

1 ½ cups peeled tomatoes
2 jalapeño peppers
½ cup chopped onions
2 tablespoons chopped fresh cilantro
sugar to taste
salt to taste
freshly ground pepper to taste
cider or red wine vinegar or juice of half a lime (optional)

In a food processor, quickly combine all of the ingredients, taking care to keep a chunky texture. For those cooks who choose to hand chop the vegetables, cut them to the desired size and place in a bowl; then add the chopped cilantro, sugar, salt, and pepper along with the optional vinegar or lime juice and blend thoroughly. Makes 2 cups.

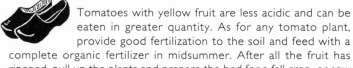

Tomatoes with yellow fruit are less acidic and can be eaten in greater quantity. As for any tomato plant, provide good fertilization to the soil and feed with a complete organic fertilizer in midsummer. After all the fruit has ripened, pull up the plants and prepare the bed for a fall crop, or sow seeds for green manure such as rye, vetch, or crimson clover.

Tomatoes Intensified

PARTIAL OVEN DRYING concentrates the flavor of fresh tomatoes, creating a texture that falls midway between a stewed tomato and a sun-dried one. Prepare as many as you can because these tomatoes will be eaten in a hurry. Plan ahead and make an extra batch for the freezer.

4 large ripe tomatoes, sliced ½ inch thick
salt to taste
freshly ground pepper to taste
3 cloves garlic, crushed
½ cup chopped fresh parsley
¼ cup olive oil

Preheat oven to 425° F. Place the tomatoes on a cookie sheet in a single layer. Sprinkle lightly with salt and pepper. In a small bowl, mix together the garlic, parsley, and olive oil. Pat this mixture on the tomatoes and bake until browned and somewhat dry, about 60 to 70 minutes. To retain the shape of the tomato slices, carefully transfer them with a spatula.

SUGGESTIONS FOR USE

Cook a pasta of your choice and add butter or olive oil, basil, and parsley. Top with the Tomatoes Intensified and sprinkle with cheese. If you have frozen the tomatoes, they can be quickly thawed and mixed with hot pasta. They are also good on spaghetti squash as an alternative to traditional sauce and on toast or crackers or as a pizza topping. They can also be used as a topping on Couscous Cauliflower Pie (page 126).

Yeast and Quick Breads

*Having to weed and weed again (and again) helps me learn patience
and acceptance; things don't have to be perfect to bear fruit.*

—A Picardo farmer

Green Tomato Tea Bread

WITH FALL COME the smell of wood smoke, the crunch of fallen leaves, crisp invigorating air—and unripened tomatoes. Never fear; green tomatoes are marvelous in this moist and spicy tea bread, sweet compensation for a cool, cloudy summer.

2 cups finely chopped
  green tomatoes
2½ cups flour
2½ teaspoons baking powder
1 teaspoon baking soda
½ teaspoon salt
1 cup brown sugar
2 tablespoons ground cinnamon
1 teaspoon freshly grated nutmeg

¼ teaspoon ground ginger
¼ teaspoon ground
  cardamom
4 tablespoons molasses
½ cup oil
2 eggs, lightly beaten
1 teaspoon vanilla
½ cup chopped walnuts

Preheat oven to 350° F. Chop the tomatoes, making sure to save all the juice. Place in a bowl and set aside. In a large bowl, sift together the flour, baking powder, baking soda, salt, sugar, cinnamon, nutmeg, ginger, and cardamom. In a separate bowl, combine the molasses, oil, eggs, vanilla, and tomatoes. Pour the tomato mixture into the dry ingredients and beat well. Add the walnuts and stir gently. Spoon the batter into two greased and floured 4-by-8-inch loaf pans. Let stand for 10 minutes before baking for 45 to 50 minutes.
Makes 2 loaves.

Tomatoes ripen from the inside out. A green tomato that has no hint of pink on the outside when the cold weather comes probably will not ripen and is best used in breads and relishes. The tomatoes with color starting to show through can be wrapped individually in paper and stored in a cool place. Once brought into a warm room, they will ripen.

Zucchini-Banana Tea Bread

GARDEN-GROWN ZUCCHINI *blended with walnuts and banana result in a sweet bread that is especially nice to present on a serving tray of assorted finger foods. Bake several mini-loaves so that you can have fresh tea breads ready on your kitchen counter and one or two tucked away in the freezer for future guests.*

½ cup butter	1½ cups all-purpose flour
1 cup sugar	½ teaspoon baking soda
½ cup dark brown sugar	2 teaspoons baking powder
2 eggs	½ teaspoon salt
1 large ripe banana, mashed	½ cup whole wheat flour
1 teaspoon vanilla	¼ cup wheat germ
1½ cups grated zucchini	½ cup chopped walnuts

Preheat oven to 350° F. In a medium bowl, cream the butter, sugar, and brown sugar until fluffy. Beat in the eggs, banana, and vanilla. Stir in the zucchini and set aside. Sift the all-purpose flour, baking soda, baking powder, and salt. Add the whole wheat flour and wheat germ to the dry ingredients and stir into the zucchini mixture. Blend thoroughly, then add the walnuts. Pour the batter into a large greased and floured 9-by-5-inch loaf pan or three to four miniloaf pans. Bake the large loaf about 70 minutes and the mini-loaves about 35 minutes. The bread should be golden brown. Makes one 9-by-5-inch loaf or 3 to 4 mini-loaves.

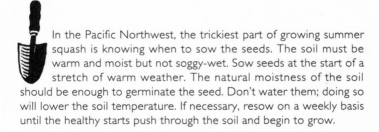

In the Pacific Northwest, the trickiest part of growing summer squash is knowing when to sow the seeds. The soil must be warm and moist but not soggy-wet. Sow seeds at the start of a stretch of warm weather. The natural moistness of the soil should be enough to germinate the seed. Don't water them; doing so will lower the soil temperature. If necessary, resow on a weekly basis until the healthy starts push through the soil and begin to grow.

Lemony Blueberry Muffins

WHAT COULD BE MORE IRRESISTIBLE than a plate full of warm blueberry muffins shining with a lemon glaze? From a hand-picked bucket of dark berries, scoop up some gems for these delectable muffins. A few crumbled lavender blossoms stirred into the muffin batter will impart a light perfume that enhances the lemon flavor.

2½ cups fresh blueberries	2 cups flour
½ cup butter, softened	2 teaspoons baking powder
1 cup sugar	¼ teaspoon salt
2 large eggs	½ cup milk
1 teaspoon vanilla	juice of 1 lemon
2 teaspoons grated lemon zest	½ cup sugar

Preheat oven to 325° F. In a small bowl, mash ½ cup of the blueberries and set aside. In a mixing bowl, cream the butter and sugar until fluffy. Beat in the eggs one at a time, then add the vanilla. Stir the mashed blueberries and lemon zest into the creamed mixture and set aside. Sift together the flour, baking powder, and salt. Slowly add the dry ingredients to the creamed mixture, alternating with the milk, and blend just until moistened. Fold in the remaining blueberries. Spoon the batter into greased muffin tins until three-quarters full and bake 25 to 30 minutes or until golden brown. To make the glaze, combine the lemon juice and sugar in a small bowl. Glaze the muffins while still warm. Cool before removing from the tins.
Makes 1 dozen muffins.

The beautiful blueberry plant, which displays bronze foliage in the spring and bright red leaves in the fall, is a good decorative choice for the landscape. An added benefit, of course, is the luscious blue fruit. Deriving from the native high bush blueberry, the plants are hardy and range in size from the 6-foot-tall varieties to 2-foot dwarfs. Their only special requirement is a well-drained acid soil with a pH of 4 to 5.

Winter Squash Waffles
with Brandy Cream

ON A LAZY WEEKEND *morning, when the snow is falling on your sleeping garden, treat yourself to a luxurious breakfast. Light, moist, and sweet spiced, these waffles are memorable mounded with billows of sweet brandied whipped cream.*

1½ cups flour

1 tablespoon baking powder

1½ teaspoons ground
   cinnamon

1 teaspoon ground ginger

½ teaspoon freshly grated
   nutmeg

⅛ teaspoon ground allspice

3 eggs, separated

1 cup milk

1½ cups cooked, mashed
   squash

1 tablespoon sugar

1 teaspoon vanilla

¼ teaspoon grated
   orange zest

¼ cup butter, melted

BRANDY CREAM TOPPING

1 cup whipping cream

1 tablespoon brandy

½ teaspoon sugar

Preheat waffle iron. In a bowl, sift together the flour, baking powder, cinnamon, ginger, nutmeg, and allspice and set aside. In a separate bowl, beat the egg yolks until lemon colored. Add the milk, squash, sugar, vanilla, and orange zest and blend together. Stir in the melted butter. Combine the dry ingredients with the squash mixture and set aside. In a ceramic or glass bowl, beat the egg whites until stiff peaks form. Gently fold the egg whites into the batter. Cook the waffles according to the instructions for your waffle iron.

To make the topping, in a chilled bowl beat the cream until it forms stiff peaks. Gently fold in the brandy and sugar. Top the hot waffles. Makes 4 large waffles.

Parsnip Breakfast Muffins

As sweet as carrots, parsnips make a superlative soft muffin spiced with mace and ginger. Mace is the dried outer seed covering of nutmeg that is similar in taste but more refined than the ground spice.

1 cup peeled, cooked, and mashed parsnips
1 egg, lightly beaten
½ cup milk
¼ cup oil
⅓ cup brown sugar
1½ cups flour
2 teaspoons baking powder
½ teaspoon ground mace
¼ teaspoon ground ginger
⅛ teaspoon salt

Preheat oven to 375° F. In a large bowl, blend the parsnips, egg, milk, oil, and sugar thoroughly and set aside. Sift together the flour, baking powder, mace, ginger, and salt. Add the dry ingredients to the parsnip mixture, gently stirring until well blended. Spoon into greased muffin tins, filling about two-thirds full. Bake for 25 minutes, until golden brown.
Makes 8 large or 12 medium muffins.

 Parsnip seed is slow to germinate, usually taking from 2 to 3 weeks. Sow in rows or broadcast, spacing seeds about 1 inch apart and ½ inch deep. Thin seedlings to 4 inches apart to allow for growth. A covering of wet burlap will help keep the soil surface moist until the seeds germinate, but it must be removed at the first sign of sprouting to allow light to the young seedlings.

Garden Muffins

THESE COLORFUL CORN MUFFINS *prove the value of a vegetable garden, to the delight of everyone's palate. Flecked with bits of orange carrots, red tomatoes, and green onions, they are especially good when served warm and spread with an herb butter of sage, garlic, and basil or topped with Hot Pepper Jelly (page 204).*

1 cup flour
1 cup yellow cornmeal
1 tablespoon sugar
2 teaspoons baking powder
½ teaspoon salt
1 egg
¾ cup milk
¼ cup oil
2 tablespoons butter, melted
½ cup peeled, seeded, and finely diced tomatoes
½ cup grated zucchini
½ cup grated carrot
¼ cup chopped green onions

Preheat oven to 400° F. In a medium bowl, combine the flour, cornmeal, sugar, baking powder, and salt and mix well. In a small bowl, beat together the egg, milk, oil, and butter. Stir in the dry ingredients. Add the tomatoes, zucchini, carrot, and green onions, blending thoroughly. Spoon the batter into greased muffin tins, filling about three-quarters full. Bake 20 to 25 minutes, until golden brown. Serve warm.
Makes 1 dozen medium muffins.

Corn Bread
with Winter Squash and Mace

CERTAIN VARIETIES OF WINTER SQUASH such as Banana, Sweet Meat, or butternut, produce a fresh, juicy puree that makes this moist, deep yellow corn bread a standout. Sweet mace lends the bread enough flavor to be served plain, but it can also be enjoyed with butter or your favorite homemade jam. Serve as an accompaniment to soup, as a light dessert, or for a late night snack.

¼ cup butter
¼ cup oil
¼ cup brown sugar
2 eggs
1½ teaspoons fresh
    lemon juice
1 cup cooked, pureed
    winter squash

¾ cup cornmeal
¾ cup whole wheat
    pastry flour
4 teaspoons baking powder
½ teaspoon ground mace
¼ cup milk

Preheat oven to 350° F. In a medium bowl, cream the butter, oil, and sugar until fluffy. Beat in the eggs and add the lemon juice and squash. Blend until very smooth and set aside. In a large bowl, thoroughly combine the cornmeal, flour, baking powder, and mace. Add the squash mixture to the dry ingredients and stir together. Add the milk and stir just until moistened. Pour into a greased 8-by-8-inch pan. Bake for 30 minutes, until golden brown.
Serves 9 to 12.

 Besides sweet corn and popcorn, other maize plants produce meal, starch, and flour, such as flint corn and dent corn (also referred to as field corn). Both types can be grown during a good summer in northern climates. Two varieties, Hooker's Sweet Indian and Black Aztec, produce blue cornmeal when grown to maturity, dried, and ground. These are both exceptional as fresh corn on the cob if picked when still white.

Herbed Biscuits

BAKING POWDER BISCUITS *become much more elegant when aromatic herbs such as rosemary or sage are added to the dough before baking. As you break open the tender hot biscuit for buttering, the steam carries a heavenly herbal fragrance into the air, inviting you to eat just one more.*

3 cups all-purpose flour
1 cup whole wheat flour
2 teaspoons sugar
2 teaspoons baking powder
1 teaspoon salt
1 teaspoon baking soda
¼ cup butter
2 tablespoons minced fresh rosemary or sage
1½ cups milk

Preheat oven to 400° F. In a bowl, combine the all-purpose flour, whole wheat flour, sugar, baking powder, salt, and baking soda. Cut in the butter and blend until the mixture is the texture of cornmeal. Stir in the rosemary or sage. Add the milk and combine to make a soft dough. Roll out the biscuits on a floured surface to ½ inch in thickness. Cut into circles and place on a greased cookie sheet, spaced about 1 inch apart. Bake for about 20 minutes, until golden brown.
Makes 2 dozen biscuits.

 Sage and rosemary are woody perennial herbs that prefer full sun, dry growing conditions, and good drainage. They are intensely flavorful; a little goes a long way. Planting a community herb garden area or sharing sprigs with neighbors is an effective way to make the most of these large plants. They can also be used ornamentally as part of an "edible landscape." Both herbs produce lavender-blue flowers in profusion.

Savory Parsnip Bread

SNIP SOME CHIVES and match them with fresh parsnips and carrots for a savory bread that complements a steaming bowl of hearty soup.

½ cup butter, softened
1 cup brown sugar
2 eggs
2 cups peeled, cooked, and mashed parsnips
½ cup grated carrots
3 tablespoons chopped fresh chives
½ cup yogurt
2 cups all-purpose flour
1 teaspoon baking soda
½ teaspoon salt
1 cup whole wheat flour

Preheat oven to 350° F. In a large bowl, cream the butter and add the brown sugar and eggs, beating until fluffy. Stir in the parsnips, carrots, chives, and yogurt and set aside. In a separate bowl, sift together the all-purpose flour, baking soda, and salt. Mix in the whole wheat flour. Combine the dry ingredients with the vegetable mixture and blend well. Spoon into two greased and floured 4-by-8-inch loaf pans. Bake for about 1 hour. Cool for 10 minutes before removing from the pans.
Makes 2 loaves.

Buying the best seed is essential for a gardener's success. Look for seed companies that offer the home gardener locally grown, field-tested, and hand-selected varieties. Such seeds have been stored in optimum conditions and should be sent promptly to arrive at your door in the freshest condition possible. When you work so hard to prepare the soil, the few extra cents spent per seed are not significant. What you want to strive for is a successful harvest.

Scones with Dried Tomatoes

MADE FAMOUS IN THE NORTHWEST *by county fairs, scones are often thought of as raspberry-filled desserts to eat while strolling the fairgrounds or as the next day's breakfast treat brought home by the bagful. These novel scones, packed with oven-dried tomatoes and garden basil, can be enjoyed anytime. Try them with cream cheese and an herb jelly or our Hot Pepper Jelly (page 204), with a slice of cheese, or just plain, steaming hot from the oven.*

2 cups flour	2 teaspoons chopped
½ cup freshly grated	fresh basil
Parmesan cheese	¾ cup chopped rehydrated
2 teaspoons baking powder	sun-dried tomatoes or
¼ teaspoon salt	drained Oven-Dried
¼ cup butter	Tomatoes (page 210)
⅓ cup milk	½ cup chopped
2 eggs	pine nuts, divided

Preheat oven to 400° F. In a medium bowl, mix the flour, Parmesan, baking powder, and salt. With a fork or pastry cutter, cut in the butter, forming a mixture that resembles cornmeal. In a separate bowl, beat together the milk, eggs, and basil. Pour the milk mixture into the flour mixture and combine thoroughly. Mix in the tomatoes and all but 2 tablespoons of the pine nuts. Gather up the dough and knead quickly for a few turns before forming into a flattened 9-inch circle. Place the dough on a greased baking sheet or in a 10-inch pie pan, cut into 8 wedges, and gently press the remaining pine nuts into the surface. Bake for 20 to 25 minutes until golden.
Makes 8 scones.

 There are numerous small fruited varieties of tomatoes bearing fruit perfect for drying. For tomato "raisins," the tiniest is aptly named Currant. Another is called Green Grape. But if you must follow tradition, Principe Borghese is the standard drying tomato used in Italy.

Herbed Vegetable Bread

WHAT COULD BE MORE SATISFYING than the smell and taste of freshly baked bread filled with your own home-grown vegetables? Lightly seasoned with dill and caraway, this bread uses a blend of wheat and rye flours and has just the right balance of delicacy and heartiness. Mix and match beets, carrots, parsnips, or potatoes for varied results.

2 tablespoons active
   dry yeast (2 packages)
½ cup lukewarm water
   (to proof)
1½ cups hot water
3 tablespoons molasses
3 tablespoons olive oil
2 teaspoons salt
3 tablespoons chopped
   fresh dill

2 teaspoons caraway seeds
2 cups finely grated root
   vegetables, such as beets,
   carrots, parsnips, or potatoes
2 cups whole wheat flour
3 to 4 cups all-purpose flour
2 cups rye flour

In a small bowl, dissolve the yeast in the lukewarm water and set aside until bubbly. In a large bowl, combine the hot water, molasses, oil, salt, dill, and caraway seeds. Stir in the grated vegetables and allow to cool slightly. When the vegetable mixture is lukewarm, add the yeast, followed by the whole wheat flour. Add 1 cup of the all-purpose flour and beat for 300 strokes. Add the rye flour and the rest of the all-purpose flour, enough to make a stiff dough. Knead on a floured board for 10 to 15 minutes. The dough should be smooth and elastic. In a greased bowl, place the dough, turn to evenly coat, cover, and allow to rise 1½ hours, until doubled. Punch down the dough and let rise another hour. Divide in two, form into loaves and place in greased loaf pans. Allow the dough to rise for 45 minutes. Preheat the oven to 375° F and bake for 35 minutes, until hollow sounding when tapped. Cool on a wire rack. Makes 2 loaves.

Italian Rosemary and Onion Bread

ITALY IS KNOWN for its fabulous food, and its crusty breads are justifiably famous. This rustic loaf is flavored by specks of chopped olives and fresh rosemary, and moistened with a garden-fresh onion.

1 tablespoon active
   dry yeast (1 package)
1 cup lukewarm water
   (to proof)
pinch of sugar
1 cup milk
½ cup cornmeal
3 tablespoons butter
1 cup chopped onions

½ cup chopped black olives
2 tablespoons chopped
   fresh rosemary
2 teaspoons salt
2 teaspoons freshly
   ground pepper
2 cups whole wheat flour
3½ to 4 cups all-purpose flour

In a small bowl, dissolve the yeast in lukewarm water with the sugar. Set aside for 5 minutes until bubbly. In a large bowl, combine the yeast, milk, cornmeal, butter, onions, olives, rosemary, salt, and pepper. Add the whole wheat flour and 2 cups of the all-purpose flour, stirring until a dough forms. Gather up the dough and knead for 10 minutes, adding the additional flour to prevent sticking. When the bread dough is elastic, turn into an oiled bowl, rotating to coat evenly. Cover and put in a warm place to rise for 1½ hours, until doubled. Punch down and divide in two. Shape into loaves and place on a baking pan sprinkled with cornmeal. Cover and set in a warm place; allow the loaves to rise for 45 minutes. Preheat the oven to 350° F and bake for 45 minutes, until crusty and hollow sounding when tapped. Cool on a wire rack.
Makes 2 loaves.

Herbed Bread Crumbs

BREAD CRUMBS ARE THE ULTIMATE *recycling recipe. Dried bread seasoned with peak-season fresh herbs from the garden is an ideal topping for vegetable casseroles and steamed vegetables. These can be used in any recipe calling for bread crumbs, such as Cheesy Vegetable Casserole (page 96) or Emerald-Stuffed Tomatoes (page 110). Certain herbs, such as basil and dill, tend to lose some of their intense fresh flavor when dried, so let the bread crumbs capture the essence of these herbs. Extend the summer freshness by storing in small plastic bags in the freezer until ready to use.*

> **assorted fresh herbs, such as thyme, oregano, basil, garlic,**
> **shallots, chives, parsley, and dill**
> **assorted stale bread slices, bagels, pita, or other flat breads**

In a food processor, place broken pieces of bread and fresh herbs. (Use ⅓ cup herbs for every 1 cup bread crumbs.) Process until the mixture is crumbly and the herbs evenly distributed. 1 average slice yields ½ to ⅔ cup crumbs.

Because our sense of smell is closely connected to our memories, harvesting herbs can be a memory-stirring occasion. Remember to pick herbs such as oregano, basil, or parsley in the "green" stage, before they flower and set seed. But herbs that are grown for seeds, such as dill, celery, and caraway, must have their flower heads left intact, or no seeds will form.

Spreads and Condiments

*It is a hidden garden in the middle of a forgotten neighborhood, a
community better known for crime and poverty and drugs. The garden is
surrounded by a 6-foot fence edged with barbed wire and locked. Outside
the fence, all appears hostile, but when I first peeked inside, I saw bright
colors: pink, orange, red, yellow, blue, and lush green.*
It is a very beautiful place, a secret garden.

—A Graham gardener

Sweet Carrot Spread

SWEET APPLE JUICE AND HONEY offset by tart lemon juice and zest awaken fresh garden-grown carrots in a beautiful orange condiment. This is a vegetable gardener's creative, low-sugar alternative to apple butter or marmalade. The grated texture of the carrots resembles that of marmalade, and the lemon flavor reinforces the illusion. It goes well on toast and nut butter sandwiches.

2 cups shredded carrots
½ cup apple juice concentrate
1 tablespoon honey
juice of half a lemon
2 teaspoons grated lemon zest

In a saucepan, combine the carrots, juice concentrate, honey, lemon juice, and zest. Bring the mixture to a boil, stirring frequently to prevent burning. Reduce the heat and simmer until thickened, stirring occasionally. After 30 minutes, test the consistency by dropping a spoonful onto a chilled plate. It should resemble jam. Store in the refrigerator in a tightly closed container.
Makes 2 cups.

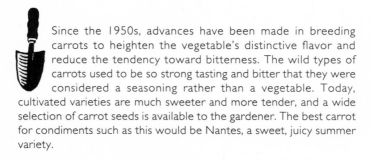

Since the 1950s, advances have been made in breeding carrots to heighten the vegetable's distinctive flavor and reduce the tendency toward bitterness. The wild types of carrots used to be so strong tasting and bitter that they were considered a seasoning rather than a vegetable. Today, cultivated varieties are much sweeter and more tender, and a wide selection of carrot seeds is available to the gardener. The best carrot for condiments such as this would be Nantes, a sweet, juicy summer variety.

Snap Bean Pâté

GARDEN-GROWN SNAP BEANS *form a smooth, creamy base for this fresh pâté. The unlikely combination of cashews and onions provides a nutty savor to the beans. This soft spread can be used in a mild form on toast or spiced up with fresh dill, garlic, curry powder, or minced hot pepper for an unsurpassed cracker spread to serve at parties. Challenge your guests to name the ingredients of this delicious pâté.*

    3 cups trimmed, chopped snap beans
    1 cup raw cashews
    1 tablespoon olive oil
    1½ cups chopped Walla Walla sweet onions or red onions
    2 teaspoons fresh lemon juice
    1 teaspoon soy sauce or tamari

In a saucepan, steam the snap beans until tender and set aside. In an small ungreased skillet, toast the cashews over medium heat until golden brown. Remove from the skillet, place in a small bowl and let cool. Pour the oil into the skillet and cook the onions until limp. Combine the snap beans, cashews, onions, lemon juice, and soy sauce or tamari in a food processor and mix together until a thick pâté consistency is reached.
Makes 4 cups.

Pole beans are efficient space saving beans and have the added benefit of a longer growing season than bush beans. The only requirements are support poles and a way to reach the beans. Scarlet runner beans and some of the purple varieties, in addition to being productive, are attractive grown over an arbor or trellis. Allowing the last "too high to reach" beans to mature will give you dry beans to use in soups or to save for next year's planting. Harvest them before fall rains or winter frosts arrive.

Nasturtium Butter

FLECKED WITH GOLD, *red, orange, magenta, burgundy, and emerald green, this flower and herb spread is a beautiful introduction to the concept of seasoned butters. Nasturtium means "nose twist"—when you are mincing the brightly colored flowers, notice the peppery smell that emanates from the flower petals and the sweet aroma that rises from its nectar. Sauté baby summer squash or other tender garden vegetables in this lovely nasturtium butter, or use on baked potatoes and breads.*

>   **20 nasturtium flowers, minced**
>   **2 shallots, minced**
>   **1 teaspoon minced fresh savory**
>   **1 teaspoon minced thyme leaves**
>   **2 teaspoons minced Italian parsley**
>   **4 tablespoons butter, softened**
>   **salt to taste**
>   **freshly ground pepper to taste**

In a small bowl, mix the minced flowers, shallots, savory, thyme, and parsley together. Add in the butter, blending thoroughly. Salt and pepper to taste. You may chill the flavored butter in a decorative mold. Refrigerate to set a shape but soften slightly before using.
Makes ½ cup.

The visual appeal of lovely flowers in a salad or a butter is yet another reason to be an organic gardener. It is important to treat your flower garden with the same earth-conscious practices that work for vegetables, not only to enjoy the edible flowers but to avoid poisoning the environment. Picking the proper plant for your particular growing conditions will help you win the battle against bugs and disease.

Honey-Pumpkin Butter

A TOUCH OF HONEY, *a suffusion of spiciness, and a drop of lemony tartness make this spread a tempting alternative to store-bought fruit butters. Did you know that honey from bees that frequent a particular type of flower take on a distinctive flavor? Awaken sleepy weekend guests with warm pancakes or crêpes topped with this flavorful homemade butter. For a change of pace, spread it on breakfast toast or in a peanut butter sandwich.*

> 2 cups cooked, pureed pumpkin
> ½ cup honey
> 1 teaspoon grated lemon zest
> 1 tablespoon fresh lemon juice
> 1 teaspoon ground cinnamon
> ⅛ teaspoon freshly grated nutmeg
> ¼ teaspoon ground ginger
> ⅛ teaspoon ground cloves
> ¼ teaspoon salt

In a saucepan, combine the pureed pumpkin with the honey, lemon zest, juice, and seasonings. Mix together and simmer, uncovered, over low heat, stirring occasionally for about 35 minutes, until the mixture is quite thick. Test the consistency by dropping a small amount of the butter onto a chilled plate. It should retain its shape and resemble jam. Store tightly covered in the refrigerator.
Makes 2 cups.

For a spring version of this spread with a lighter lemony lift, increase the lemon zest to 2 teaspoons. Leave out the cinnamon, nutmeg, ginger, and cloves. The type of honey used will affect the flavor as well; a pale honey would be best for this springtime variation.

Cilantro Chutney

COMMONLY ASSOCIATED WITH EAST INDIAN and Chinese cuisines, cilantro and coriander were believed by the ancient Romans and Persians to promote digestion, longevity, and a good love life. This recipe is unabashedly wild and flavorful. Enjoy it with pita bread or rice pilaf.

¼ cup fresh lemon juice

¼ cup water

2 cups chopped, packed cilantro

¼ cup finely grated fresh coconut

¼ cup finely chopped onions

2 tablespoons grated fresh ginger

2 tablespoons chopped jalapeño pepper

1 teaspoon sugar

½ teaspoon salt

¼ teaspoon freshly ground pepper

In a food processor, mix the lemon juice, water, and half of the cilantro until reduced to a puree. Gradually add the rest of the cilantro, blending after each addition. Add the coconut, onions, ginger, jalapeño pepper, sugar, salt, and pepper and blend thoroughly.
Makes 2 cups.

In cool weather, cilantro is a bushy, low-growing plant, not more than 8 inches in height. The lengthening of the days and rising temperatures trigger the plant to begin flowering. The herb's flavor diminishes quickly when the plant starts to change from the leafy bush to a 3-foot-tall flowering form. Use up the greens and soft stems quickly because they don't retain their flavor when dry. If you allow the plant to flower and form seeds, the result is the spice coriander. Use these seeds in their green stage for Thai cuisine, or grind them when dry to use in curry or in cookies, cakes, and gingerbreads.

Red Tomato Chutney

CHUTNEYS ARE CONDIMENTS *consisting of fruits or vegetables slowly simmered in vinegar and flavored with a touch of sweetness and spiciness. They make marvelous marinades and cooking sauces to use with vegetables that are quickly cooked on the grill. The tomatoes in this chutney blend beautifully with the cinnamon and cumin, giving a special Middle Eastern flavor to piping hot rice or orzo as well as steamed vegetables such as cauliflower. This stores well in the freezer.*

1 tablespoon butter
1 tablespoon oil
2 whole jalapeño peppers, dried or fresh
1 teaspoon cumin seeds
1-inch stick of cinnamon
2 cups coarsely chopped tomatoes
3 tablespoons brown sugar
½ teaspoon salt

In a large skillet, heat the butter and oil over medium heat. When hot but not smoking, add the jalapeño peppers, cumin seeds, and cinnamon stick. Sauté the mixture until the seeds turn brown. Stir in the tomatoes, brown sugar, and salt. Continue cooking, stirring occasionally, about 10 to 15 minutes, until the chutney is reduced to a thickened consistency.
Makes 1 cup.

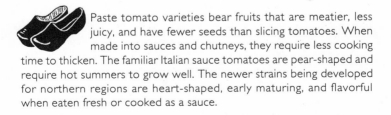

Paste tomato varieties bear fruits that are meatier, less juicy, and have fewer seeds than slicing tomatoes. When made into sauces and chutneys, they require less cooking time to thicken. The familiar Italian sauce tomatoes are pear-shaped and require hot summers to grow well. The newer strains being developed for northern regions are heart-shaped, early maturing, and flavorful when eaten fresh or cooked as a sauce.

Cambodian Pickled Vegetables

CULTURAL DIFFERENCES *don't seem to present a problem to gardener-cooks who share a love of growing their own fresh vegetables and enjoying them for as many seasons as possible. Remarkably easy to prepare, this simple recipe uses a traditional Southeast Asian method for pickling many types of garden vegetables, such as Chinese cabbage, turnips, carrots, green onions, and cucumbers. By slightly varying the amounts of vinegar, salt, and sugar in a batch, sweeter or sourer versions will result. It is best to use only one type of vegetable in a batch, but don't be afraid to try different vegetables.*

> **3 cups chopped vegetables**
> **1 tablespoon vinegar**
> **1 tablespoon salt**
> **1 tablespoon sugar**
> **boiling water**

Fill a 1-quart jar with the vegetables and add the vinegar, salt, and sugar. Pour boiling water into the jar, filling three-quarters full. Place a lid loosely on the jar and set in the sun or a warm place. Check daily to observe the fermentation and, if necessary, move to a warmer place to speed up the process. After three days, the vegetables should be fermented and have developed a pickled taste. When the vegetables obtain the desired flavor, cover tightly, and refrigerate. Use within three weeks.
Makes 1 quart.

Only a few of the many Asian vegetables are available in local markets, but gardeners can grow myriad types of vegetables if they are willing to search out the seeds and meet the challenge of growing something different. It can be an adventure to learn all the plants' names and then to find a seed company that offers what you want to try. Finding an experienced gardener is the best way to learn firsthand how to grow new vegetables. A community garden offers the advantage of access to people from all backgrounds and experiences who are willing to share their knowledge.

Parsley Gremolata

GREMOLATA IS A TRADITIONAL ITALIAN *condiment that takes advantage of the naturally complementary ingredients of fresh parsley and lemon. Simple to make, this fine-textured, brilliant green topping can be used on almost anything—as a spread on crackers or crusty French bread, as a topping on steamed vegetables or stuffed baked potatoes, or as an accent for any main course.*

1½ cups finely chopped fresh parsley
4 cloves garlic, minced
3 tablespoons grated lemon zest

In a medium bowl, combine the parsley, garlic, and lemon zest. Allow the gremolata's ingredients to commingle at room temperature for several hours. As with a marinade, time will enhance the flavors.
Makes 1½ cups.

Parsley grows easily, but it is especially important to use fresh seed and sow early in spring. Having a good soil nitrogen content will ensure success. Pale, light green, or slow-growing plants can benefit from a side dressing of blood meal or other high-nitrogen source. Parsley is biennial, meaning it blooms in the second year. Harvest the lower leafy portion for best flavor before it blooms. For a continuous supply of parsley plants, allow one to go to seed.

Horseradish Dip

THE TANGY HOT ROOT of horseradish is an important enhancement to many cuisines around the world. Because of its hot esters, preparation, though simple, is best done outside or near an open window. Keep your hands away from your eyes at all times. Store prepared raw horseradish in the refrigerator and you will have a superb seasoning to add to sauces, dips, dressings, and stuffings. This easy, lively dip is best served chilled with sliced fresh garden vegetables.

½ cup minced green onions
3 tablespoons prepared horseradish (recipe follows)
2 tablespoons minced chives
1½ cups yogurt
salt to taste
freshly ground pepper to taste

In a food processor, combine all ingredients and blend until smooth. Makes 1½ cups.

PREPARED HORSERADISH

In a bowl with enough white wine vinegar, distilled vinegar, or lemon juice to keep the horseradish root covered, grate the peeled horseradish root. (Do not use cider vinegar; it will discolor the root.) Quickly transfer to a clean storage jar that will be completely filled with the horseradish and screw on a tight-fitting lid to reduce exposure to air, which causes discoloration. The tanginess will be strongest for about three weeks.

The somewhat invasive horseradish plant is characterized by elongated shiny green leaves atop large, deep tap roots. One plant is usually enough for an average family's consumption, and once planted, it is difficult to eradicate. A piece of the tap root is all that is needed to propagate horseradish, either on purpose by planting the tap root in the spring or by accident when pieces of the root remain in the soil after fall harvests. The tap root grows larger in the late summer to early fall; wait until October or November to harvest it.

Desserts

*I love digging in the dirt and making lakes and houses
with mud, and running through the sprinkler when it's hot. I also like
riding in the wheelbarrow on the way back from bringing things to the
compost. And when Laura and I go to get the wheelbarrows, we play train
and make up names for different train stops. Laura rides, I push.
We love to run up and down the paths. I like raiding the compost for dead
flowers to play flower fairies with and taking calendula flowers and
maybe adding poppy seeds as flavoring, but definitely adding water
because that is fairy tea. I'm glad we have a P-Patch.*

—A young Picardo farmer

Berry Sorbet

REFRESHING SORBETS *are popular nondairy frozen desserts made from lemon, sugar, and various kinds of fruit. Here is a standard recipe that can be altered to fit your harvest of raspberries, blackberries, blueberries, or strawberries. The amount of sugar can be adjusted to fit both the sweetness of the fruit and your individual taste, but the lemon is necessary to bring out the flavor of the fruit. Créme de cassis, orange liqueur, or even Anisette will make your sorbet truly exceptional.*

>   2 cups water
>   1¾ cups sugar
>   3 tablespoons fresh lemon juice
>   1½ tablespoons berry liqueur
>   6 cups berries, pureed and sieved

In a medium saucepan, combine the water and sugar. Over low heat, stir to dissolve the sugar. Bring to a boil and cook for 2 minutes. Remove from heat and stir in the lemon and liqueur. Pour into a medium bowl and refrigerate to cool. When the syrup is completely cool (or refrigerated up to 3 days), stir in the sieved pulp. Either freeze the mixture in an ice cube tray until almost solid and whisk the cubes into a smooth consistency, or process in an ice cream maker according to the directions. Freeze the sorbet until firm, about 1 hour, before serving. If frozen solid, allow it to soften slightly in the refrigerator.

Makes 1½ quarts.

Golden-fruited raspberries were developed by crossing such red bearing plants as Taylor and Fall Red with a wild Korean berry. Black raspberries or blackcaps are shrublike, nonsuckering plants related to red raspberries. They have a distinctive flavor and a seedier berry. Brandywine and Sodus are two varieties of raspberries with purple fruit arising from crosses between the red and black raspberry.

THE CITY GARDENER'S COOKBOOK

Raspberry Mousse

FRESH RASPBERRIES ARE REDUCED *to a thick pulp, slightly sweetened, and expanded with plenty of whipped cream. Rich and luxurious, this delightful pink mousse is attractive garnished with whole fresh berries, a glossy green leaf, and a strip of lime zest. Blackberries, blueberries, or loganberries work equally well.*

3 cups raspberries

2 egg yolks

2 teaspoons sugar

1 cup whipping cream

lime zest and whole berries, for garnish

In a double boiler, cook the washed raspberries, egg yolks, and sugar, stirring for 10 minutes until thickened. Refrigerate the mixture for 1 hour until firm. In a small bowl, whip the cream into stiff peaks, then stir a small part of the whipped cream into the raspberry mixture. Fold the entire raspberry mixture back into the whipped cream. Divide into individual serving dishes and garnish. Serves 6.

 Raspberries are biennial plants. The flowers and fruit generally develop the second year on canes grown the previous year. The exception is the autumn-fruiting varieties, which have a second harvest period in the fall. When raspberries have finished bearing, prune out the old dead canes and feed the new canes. This allows the new canes to grow up strong and lowers the chances of overwintering diseases.

Gooseberry Fool

FOOL IS A DESSERT *made of crushed, stewed fruit mixed with cream or custard and served cold. Try this updated version using sugared garden-grown gooseberries or currants suspended in silky yogurt and whipped cream. For best results, serve within 4 hours after making.*

2 cups vanilla yogurt
2 cups gooseberries
¾ cup sugar
1 tablespoon water
½ teaspoon rose water
½ cup whipping cream

Reduce the liquid in the yogurt by placing it in a colander and draining for 1 hour. In a saucepan, cook the cleaned gooseberries, sugar, and water over medium heat for 5 to 10 minutes, or until soft. Puree the berry mixture and press through a sieve. Add rose water and chill in the refrigerator until cold. When the drained yogurt measures 1½ cups, place in a bowl and stir to even out the texture. Lightly swirl the gooseberries into the yogurt. In a chilled bowl, whip the cream until stiff and gently fold into the berries and yogurt. Spoon into individual dessert cups and serve immediately. Serves 6.

Although Americans are less familiar with gooseberries, the fruit is highly prized in Europe. The green translucent berries grow on 4-foot-high thorny bushes and ripen in July. Although they are considered a tart cooking berry, cultivated varieties selected for sweetness can be eaten straight from the bush after they turn red. The plants require full sun, well-drained soil, and annual pruning. After 2 years, you can look forward to a crop of berries.

Red Raspberry Flummery

A SOFT, JAMLIKE DESSERT, *flummery is closest to a pudding in consistency. This version, with its intense raspberry flavor, is good plain or sweetened with vanilla ice cream. The Pacific Northwest is famous for its berries and fruit liqueurs—so experiment with loganberries, currants, marionberries, tayberries, and boysenberries. For extra smoothness with large-seeded berries, consider sieving the puree before cooking.*

3 ½ cups raspberry puree
1 tablespoon fresh lemon juice
1 cup water
¾ cup sugar
⅓ cup quick-cooking tapioca
3 tablespoons fruit liqueur or fresh orange juice
3 ½ teaspoons grated lemon zest
½ teaspoon vanilla
sweet woodruff blossoms and leaves, violas,
   Johnny-jump-ups, or borage blossoms, for garnish

In a saucepan, combine the raspberry puree, lemon juice, water, sugar, and tapioca. Let stand for 5 minutes to allow the tapioca to soften. Cook the mixture over medium-high heat until it boils, stirring continuously. Remove from heat and add in the fruit liqueur or orange juice, lemon zest, and vanilla. Cool slightly and transfer into small serving bowls. Cover and refrigerate until set. Garnish with flowers.
Serves 6.

Sugar Plum Soufflé

THE VENERABLE ITALIAN PLUM TREE in the back corner of the Pine-hurst P-Patch provides much-appreciated grazing food at the garden and excellent dried plums. Low in fat and light in texture, this delici-ous dessert is ideal for the holidays. If you don't have access to fresh plums and a food drier, you can use packaged prunes. You'll have the best success with this and any other soufflé if your eggs are at room temperature.

  1 cup dried Italian plums or prunes, chopped
  ⅓ cup apple juice concentrate
  1 tablespoon orange liqueur or lemon juice
  1 teaspoon orange or lemon zest
  3 egg whites
  ¼ teaspoon salt
  ¼ cup brown sugar
  ½ cup finely chopped pecans

Soak prune pieces in the juice concentrate and liqueur or lemon juice to rehydrate. Heat gently for 5 minutes to expedite the process or soak them overnight. Puree with any excess liquid until smooth. Preheat the oven to 350° F. In a ceramic or glass bowl, beat the egg whites, adding the salt and brown sugar, 1 tablespoon at a time, until stiff peaks form. Gently fold the prune mixture and pecans into the egg whites. Pour into an ungreased 1½-quart soufflé dish or casserole and set into a pan of hot water. Bake for 30 to 35 minutes, until golden brown.
Serves 4 to 6.

Pudding in Your Pumpkin

THIS TRADITIONAL HMONG RECIPE *is a charming way to use mini-pumpkins and can be varied by filling the pumpkins with fruit compote or bread or rice pudding.*

8 miniature pumpkins
5 eggs, beaten
½ cup sugar
1 cup coconut milk

Preheat oven to 350° F. Carefully cut the tops from the pumpkins and set aside to use later. Scoop out and discard the seeds. Place the pumpkin shells in a 9-by-13-inch baking pan. In a bowl, combine the eggs, sugar, and coconut milk. Pour the mixture into the pumpkins and put the tops back on. Place the pumpkins in the oven with a pan of water on the rack below. Bake for 45 minutes, until set.
Serves 8.

It is hard to explain the attraction we all have to the golden-orange fruits of the pumpkin plant. Jack-Be-Little is one variety of the new tiny pumpkins popular with kids of all ages. They are only 3 to 4 inches across, but because the plants set an abundance of these sweet and flavorful fruits, you will have enough to eat and to use for a holiday centerpiece decoration. Grow mini-pumpkins like other pumpkins, sowing the seed when the weather warms, and harvesting before frost.

Blackberry Crumble

LADEN WITH FRUIT, WILD BLACKBERRY *bushes seem to appear every-where you turn in the Pacific Northwest in late summer. The happy harvester fills buckets to the brim with luscious purple-black berries and then wonders what to do with the treasure. A classic blackberry cobbler rewards those who are able to save some of the fruit from being eaten as fast as it is picked. Served warm with a dollop of ice cream, yogurt, or sour cream atop the bubbling juices, this dessert has to be the most fitting finale to a summer evening with friends.*

5 cups blackberries
2 tablespoons flour
sugar to taste
½ cup butter, softened
1 cup rolled oats
½ cup all-purpose flour
½ cup whole wheat flour
1 cup brown sugar

Preheat oven to 350° F. Rinse the blackberries and remove stems. Place the berries in a deep 8-by-8-inch baking dish, filling to within 1 inch of the top. Gently stir in the flour to thicken the juices and sprinkle the berries with sugar. Set aside. In a bowl, combine the butter, oats, flours, and brown sugar to make a crumbly texture. Place on top of the berries and pat lightly. Bake for 30 to 35 minutes, until juice starts to bubble around the edges. Serve warm with ice cream, yogurt, or sour cream.
Serves 6.

There are thornless varieties available of blackberries and loganberries. The loganberry, thought to be a cross between the red raspberry and the blackberry, has a large flavorful fruit but is not as productive as the marionberry or the tayberry. There are crosses between loganberries and wild blackberries as well as with black raspberries. No matter the color or size, if the center core stays with the fruit when picked, it is part of the blackberry family.

Rhubarb Cobbler

WHILE ASSEMBLING THIS COBBLER you can look forward to sweet fruit bubbling up around the edges of a golden brown dough when it comes hot out of the oven. The tart rhubarb is subtly flavored with cinnamon, ginger, and orange zest. You can vary the fruit filling; try using berries, apples, pears, peaches, or apricots. Because the sweetness of the fruit differs, you'll need to adjust the amount of sugar accordingly.

5 cups chopped rhubarb
1 tablespoon grated orange zest
1 cup granulated sugar, divided
1 cup flour
½ cup oatmeal
¼ teaspoon salt
3 teaspoons baking powder
¼ teaspoon cream of tartar
1 teaspoon ground cinnamon
½ teaspoon ground ginger
½ cup brown sugar
1 egg
½ cup milk
5 tablespoons butter, melted

Preheat oven to 400° F. In a large bowl, combine the rhubarb, orange zest, and ⅔ cup of the granulated sugar. Set aside. In a separate bowl, stir together the flour, oatmeal, salt, baking powder, cream of tartar, cinnamon, ginger, and brown sugar. In a third bowl, beat the egg with the milk and melted butter. Combine the liquid mixture with the flour mixture. Place the rhubarb in a greased 9-by-13-inch pan. Spread the dough over the rhubarb and sprinkle with the remaining granulated sugar. Bake for 25 to 30 minutes, until golden brown and bubbly.
Serves 8.

Rhubarb is a bold herbaceous perennial that grows up to 5 feet tall. The dark green leaves are huge, up to 1½ feet across. With its contrasting red stalk, rhubarb is an attractive addition in sunny or shady landscape beds and container plantings.

Red, White, and Blue Berry Tart with Red Currant Glaze

The "RED, WHITE, AND BLUE" month of July is the time of year when luscious berries thickly pack the bushes. The best way to have access to the ever-fragile berries in prime condition is to grow them yourself. Planting any of the early varieties of blueberries, some early- to mid-season raspberries, and a few white alpine strawberries will allow you to pick a bowl of sweet, tricolor berries. This festive summer tart, with a crust sparked with gingersnaps, shows off your harvest in style. Artfully arrange the fruit, coat with a currant glaze, add a cap of whipped cream, and you won't have to set off fireworks to hear oohs and aahs.

1 ½ cups crushed gingersnaps
3 tablespoons butter, softened
1 egg, lightly beaten
5 cups mixed fresh berries
2 cups Red Currant Glaze (recipe follows)
whipping cream (optional)

Preheat oven to 350° F. To prepare the crust, mix the gingersnaps, butter, and egg in a bowl until evenly moist and crumbly. On a 12-inch pizza pan with sides or tart pan, firmly press the mixture across the bottom and up the sides. Bake for about 10 minutes, until the edges are brown. Set aside to cool completely. Rinse and drain the berries just before assembling the tart, then carefully arrange them on the crust. Prepare the glaze by warming it over low heat until thinned to a flowing consistency. Spoon or brush the warmed glaze evenly over the fruit in a thin layer. Cool the tart before serving. Serves 8 to 10.

RED CURRANT GLAZE

2 cups pureed fresh currants

4 tablespoons sugar

In a heavy saucepan, boil the currants and sugar together until thick and the mixture forms a thread when drizzled from a spoon (228° F on a candy thermometer). If the glaze is made ahead of time, cover and keep refrigerated. When ready to use, set the glaze over hot water until it is warm and can be easily drizzled over the tart. If after warming it is too thick, a few hot water droplets can be added and stirred until it is the proper consistency.
Makes 2 cups.

 A hardy plant of the genus *Ribes,* currants have vitamin C–packed fruit that is good for jams and glazes. Currants are also good to eat plain when ripe, or they can be dried like raisins. There are varieties with red, black, and even white berries. Plant them 4 feet apart in a sunny location and top the root area with a mulch of compost. The 3- to 5-foot bushes need to be pruned in order to keep them open and airy in the center to help discourage diseases. After 2 years, fruiting will begin, and the plant will continue to bear for 15 to 30 years if properly cared for.

Strawberry-Rhubarb Custard Pie

EVERY YEAR THERE COMES A MAGICAL DAY when suddenly the world is new and green and it is time to say thank you for the first spring harvest of strawberries and rhubarb.

PIE CRUST

> **2 cups chilled pastry flour**
> **⅔ cup chilled butter**
> **1 egg, lightly beaten**
> **4 to 5 tablespoons cold water**

In a medium bowl, cut the butter into the flour with a fork or pastry cutter until the texture is the consistency of cornmeal. Add in the egg, and then gradually add the water, one tablespoon at a time, working the dough until it forms a ball. Divide in half for a 9-inch double crust. Chill before rolling.
Makes one 9-inch double crust or one 10-inch single crust and 3 tartlets.

FILLING

> **3 eggs, lightly beaten**
> **1 to 1½ cups sugar**
> **4 tablespoons flour**
> **3 cups halved strawberries**
> **3 cups rhubarb, cut into ½-inch pieces**

Preheat the oven to 400° F. Roll out the bottom crust and place in a 9-inch pie pan. In a large bowl, lightly beat the eggs and add in the sugar and flour. Stir in the strawberries and rhubarb. Pour into the crust-filled pie pan. Roll out the top crust and drape over the pie, shaping the sides. Cut slits into the top crust to allow steam to escape while baking. Place in the oven on a middle rack with an overflow baking sheet on the lower rack. Bake for 45 minutes. Serves 6 to 8.

Sweet Winter Squash Pie

TRADITIONAL PUMPKIN PIE *cooling on the counter is a familiar sight in the kitchen, but the gardener-cook has the advantage of using a variety of winter squash to blend into a smooth, spicy custard. Sweet Meat and butternut are two good choices, but don't limit yourself. Fill your home with the sweet smell of a freshly baked squash pie. Serve each slice with a dollop of whipped cream.*

1 10-inch single pie crust, unbaked (see recipe under
   Strawberry-Rhubarb Custard Pie, page 186)
3 cups cooked, pureed winter squash
2 tablespoons molasses
¾ cup honey
¼ teaspoon ground cloves
3 teaspoons ground cinnamon
1½ teaspoons ground ginger
½ teaspoon salt
4 eggs, lightly beaten
1½ cups cream

Preheat oven to 400° F. In a large bowl, combine the squash, molasses, honey, cloves, cinnamon, ginger, salt, eggs, and cream. Mix until completely smooth. Pour the filling into the prepared pie crust and bake for 10 minutes. Reduce the heat to 350° F and bake for another 45 minutes, until the custard is set.
Serves 8 to 10.

Winter squash is a vigorous plant that many people grow over trellises to save space. A common problem is that the developing fruit is heavy and needs support. P-Patch gardens offer a condensed view of how different people solve the same problem. Some common supports have included cloth slings, nylon stockings, wooden crosspieces, or upside-down coffee cans. The prize for the most creative support went to a gardener who built a seated scarecrow with a lap in just the right place.

Back to Your Roots Cookies

THIS RECIPE has been in the P-Patch family for 20 years and is served at many a work party when fall is in the air. The cookies are light, soft, and cakelike, with a tangy orange frosting. Beets can be substituted for the carrots and will turn your cookies pink.

1 cup butter	FROSTING
¾ cup sugar	1 tablespoon butter
1 cup cooked, mashed carrots	1 cup confectioners' sugar
1 egg	juice of half an orange
1 teaspoon vanilla	zest of 1 orange, grated
2 cups flour	
2 teaspoons baking powder	
½ teaspoon salt	
¼ teaspoon freshly grated nutmeg	
⅛ teaspoon ground cardamom	

Preheat oven to 350° F. In a medium bowl, cream the butter and sugar until fluffy. Beat in the mashed carrots, egg, and vanilla, and set aside. In a separate bowl, sift the flour, baking powder, salt, nutmeg, and cardamom. Add the dry ingredients to the carrot mixture and blend thoroughly. Drop by heaping teaspoons onto a greased cookie sheet. Bake for 20 minutes or until light golden brown.

To make frosting, in a small bowl cream the butter with the sugar. Add the juice and zest and blend thoroughly. Frost the cookies while they are slightly warm.
Makes 30 cookies.

Golden Carrot-Oatmeal Cookies

CARROTS, RAISINS, NUTS, AND ORANGE ZEST *make a longstanding favorite, the oatmeal cookie, a true delight. Cinnamon, nutmeg, ginger, and allspice flavor these wholesome treats for your cookie jar.*

⅓ cup butter	½ teaspoon ground cinnamon
⅓ cup brown sugar	¼ teaspoon freshly grated
⅓ cup molasses	nutmeg
¼ cup honey	½ teaspoon ground allspice
2 eggs	¼ teaspoon ground ginger
1 cup grated carrots	½ cup whole wheat flour
1½ cups all-purpose flour	1 teaspoon grated orange zest
2 teaspoons baking powder	2 cups rolled oats
¼ teaspoon baking soda	1 cup raisins
¼ teaspoon salt	½ cup chopped walnuts

Preheat oven to 350° F. In a large bowl, cream the butter and add the brown sugar, molasses, and honey until fluffy. Add the eggs, beating after each addition until smooth. Stir in the carrots and set aside. In a separate bowl, sift together the all-purpose flour, baking powder, soda, salt, cinnamon, nutmeg, allspice, and ginger. Mix in the whole wheat flour, orange zest, and oats. Add the dry ingredients to the carrot mixture, combining thoroughly. Blend in the raisins and nuts. Drop by rounded teaspoons onto a greased cookie sheet and bake until golden, about 15 minutes. Transfer the hot cookies to a rack to cool.
Makes 3 to 4 dozen.

Oats, though not practical to grow as a food crop in the home garden, make a dramatic addition to the list of unusual ornamental plants. They are a tall clumping grass with attractive oat-groat seed heads.

Candied Flowers

CANDIED FLOWERS *hold their fresh shape and bright color under a glistening coat of fine sugar crystals and make lovely accents for desserts and cakes. The blooms traditionally used are members of the viola family, including pansies, violets, and Johnny-jump-ups, but any organically grown edible flower will work well. You will need a small paintbrush, a pair of tweezers, and a wire rack. The best time to harvest the flowers is in the morning after the dew has dried. Select perfect blossoms at their visual peak, leaving ¼ inch of stem to make handling easier.*

1 egg white
2 dozen fresh flowers, gently washed and dried
½ cup fine granulated sugar

In a bowl, beat the egg white until it is frothy. Use the brush to paint the egg white onto the top and bottom of each petal. Hold the flower by the stem with the tweezers and either dip the flowers in the sugar or lightly sprinkle the sugar onto each petal. If you are using large multipetaled flowers, you will need to carefully pull the flower apart, painting and coating each petal separately. They can be easily reassembled when you are ready to use them. Place each candied flower on a wire rack; put in a cool, dark location and let dry until the sugar has hardened. Store the flowers in an airtight container for up to a year.

There are at least 50 edible flowers that grow in the Pacific Northwest. Make sure to identify them correctly so as to avoid poisonous look-alikes. Some candidates for crystallizing include apple blossoms, borage, single-flowered dianthus species, scented geraniums, fairy roses, Johnny-jump-ups, lemon marigolds, pansies, and violets, baby gladiolus, scarlet runner beans, and Chinese snow pea blossoms (not sweet peas, which are poisonous).

THE CITY GARDENER'S COOKBOOK

Rich Classic Carrot Cake
with Cream Cheese Frosting

FRESHLY GRATED CARROTS *make all the difference in this spicy cake.*

2 cups flour
2 teaspoons baking soda
2 cups sugar
1 teaspoon salt
2 teaspoons ground cinnamon
4 eggs, lightly beaten
1 ½ cups oil
3 cups grated carrots
1 ½ cups chopped walnuts
lemon marigold blossoms, calendula petals,
   or ginger mint sprigs, for garnish

CREAM CHEESE FROSTING

8 ounces cream cheese, softened
1 ½ cups butter
3 ½ cups confectioners' sugar (1 pound)
2 teaspoons vanilla

Preheat oven to 350° F. In a bowl, sift together the flour, baking soda, sugar, salt, and cinnamon. In a separate large bowl, whisk the eggs and the oil, then stir in the carrots and walnuts. Add the dry ingredients into the carrot mixture, blending until evenly moist. Pour into a greased and floured 9-by-13-inch cake pan and bake for 30 to 40 minutes.

To make the frosting, in a bowl mix the softened cream cheese and butter. Add the sugar and vanilla and blend until smooth. Frost the cake after it has cooled. Garnish with flowers or mint sprigs. Serves 15 to 20.

Carrot Cake with Fruit

THIS SPICY CAKE IS PLUMP with fruits and nuts. The prunes, carrots, and pineapple lend enough sweetness so that no frosting is needed. Look closely; there is no oil in the recipe, making it a good choice for those who want the cake but not the calories.

1 cup chopped prunes
6 tablespoons hot fruit juice (orange, apple, or pear)
¼ cup chopped walnuts
2½ cups cake flour
2 teaspoons baking powder
1½ teaspoons baking soda
2 teaspoons ground cinnamon
1 egg yolk
1½ cups sugar
2 cups grated carrots
1 cup crushed, drained pineapple
3 egg whites
pineapple mint sprigs, pineapple sage leaves,
   or chamomile blossoms, for garnish

Preheat oven to 350° F. Puree the prunes and the hot juice until smooth and set aside to cool. Sprinkle the walnuts evenly in a shallow baking pan, toast them until golden brown and set aside. In a medium bowl, sift together the flour, baking powder, baking soda, and cinnamon. In a large bowl, whisk the egg yolk, then mix in the sugar, carrots, pineapple, and prune puree. Set aside. Whip the egg whites in a glass or ceramic bowl until stiff. Add the fruit mixture to the dry ingredients, mixing until evenly moist. Gently fold in the egg whites and walnuts. Pour into a greased and floured bundt cake pan and bake about 45 minutes. Garnish with flowers or herbs.
Serves 10 to 12.

Carob Zucchini Cake
with Creamy Coffee Glaze

HARD TO BELIEVE *though it may be, not everyone lives for chocolate.
This zucchini cake with carob powder tastes like a rich gingerbread that
everyone can enjoy, rather than a would-be chocolate cake. For a low-
fat alternative, substitute one cup of yogurt for the butter and eggs,
and dust with confectioners' sugar instead of using the glaze.*

¾ cup butter

1½ cups brown sugar

3 eggs

2 teaspoons vanilla

½ cup carob powder

2 cups coarsely grated zucchini

2½ cups flour

2½ teaspoons baking powder

1½ teaspoons baking soda

½ teaspoon salt

¼ teaspoon ground cinnamon

½ cup milk

1 cup chopped walnuts

cinnamon or lemon basil
   leaves and flowers, (non-
   edible flowers, remove
   before eating), for garnish

CREAMY COFFEE GLAZE

1 cup carob chips

¼ cup whipping cream

2 tablespoons strong coffee

Preheat oven to 350° F. In a large bowl, cream the butter and sugar
together. Add the eggs, one at a time, and beat until the mixture is
fluffy. Stir in the vanilla, carob powder, and zucchini. In a separate
bowl, sift together the flour, baking powder, baking soda, salt, and
cinnamon. Alternately stir the dry ingredients and the milk into
the zucchini mixture. Fold in the nuts. Pour into a greased and
floured bundt cake pan and bake for 1 hour. Allow the cake to cool
for 15 minutes before inverting onto a rack.

To make the glaze, in a double boiler melt the carob chips and
set aside. In a separate pan, bring the cream to a boil, add the
melted carob, and whisk together. Stir in the coffee and continue
to whisk until blended. Drizzle the glaze over the warm cake.
Garnish with flowers.
Serves 10 to 12.

Fudgy Orange-Zucchini Cake
with Orange Glaze

THIS DENSE CHOCOLATE CAKE, *drizzled with orange glaze, is always a favorite at the annual P-Patch harvest banquet.*

2½ cups flour
½ cup cocoa
2½ teaspoons baking powder
1½ teaspoons baking soda
1 teaspoon salt
1 teaspoon ground cinnamon
¾ cup butter
2 cups sugar
3 eggs, lightly beaten
2 teaspoons vanilla
½ cup milk
3 cups grated zucchini
1 tablespoon grated
   orange zest

1 cup chopped nuts
calendula blossoms
   and petals, tuberous
   begonia blossoms,
   or orange mint sprigs,
   for garnish

ORANGE GLAZE
1¼ cups sifted
   confectioners' sugar
¼ cup fresh orange juice
1 teaspoon vanilla

Preheat oven to 350° F. Sift the flour, cocoa, baking powder, baking soda, salt, and cinnamon together and set aside. In a bowl, cream the butter and sugar until fluffy. Add the eggs, vanilla, and milk to the butter mixture. Stir in the dry ingredients and mix until well blended. Fold in the zucchini, orange zest, and nuts. Pour into a greased and floured bundt cake pan. Bake 50 to 60 minutes. Allow the cake to cool for 15 minutes before turning out onto a rack.

To make the glaze, in a bowl mix together the sugar, orange juice, and vanilla. While the cake is still warm, drizzle with the glaze. Garnish with flowers or mint sprigs.
Serves 10 to 12.

Raspberry Brownies

CHOCOLATE and raspberries. Need we say more?

8 ounces unsweetened chocolate
1 cup butter
5 eggs
1 tablespoon vanilla
1 teaspoon almond extract
$\frac{1}{8}$ teaspoon salt
$\frac{1}{4}$ cup strong coffee
3 cups sugar
$1\frac{3}{4}$ cup flour
$1\frac{1}{2}$ cups chopped walnuts
3 cups red raspberries, divided

Preheat oven to 425° F. In a double boiler, melt the chocolate and butter, stirring occasionally. Remove from heat and set aside. In a large bowl, thoroughly beat the eggs, vanilla, almond extract, salt, coffee, and sugar until smooth. Then stir in the chocolate mixture. Add the flour and blend lightly. Stir in the nuts. Spread the batter into a greased and floured 9-by-13-inch baking pan. Sprinkle 2 cups of the raspberries over the batter. Press the raspberries lightly into the top of the batter, then bake for 30 to 35 minutes. Let stand until cool, cut into squares, and serve topped with the remaining raspberries. The brownies can be served hot with a scoop of vanilla ice cream.
Serves 15 to 20.

Chocolate Beet Cake
with Rich Chocolate Frosting

HARVEST YOUR FRESH BEETS *with a new destination in mind. An exquisite dark chocolate cake enriched with beets doesn't seem contradictory when you remember that beet roots are one of the main sources of sugar. The burgundy roots deepen the color of the cake; the puree makes it dense and moist; and the beets' earthy sweetness combines perfectly with chocolate. The fluffy chocolate frosting is decadently rich. Serve this cake to your chocolate-loving friends and let them wonder what makes it so good.*

1½ cups cooked, peeled, and pureed beets

3 ounces unsweetened chocolate

3 eggs

1½ cups sugar

1 cup oil

1 teaspoon vanilla

1¾ cups flour

1½ teaspoons baking soda

¼ teaspoon salt

red, white, or pink roses with sweet woodruff blossoms,
    red roses with French lavender blossoms, or
    gladiolus blossoms, for garnish

RICH CHOCOLATE FROSTING

2 ounces unsweetened chocolate

¾ cup butter

1 cup sugar

1 teaspoon vanilla

¼ cup flour

1 cup milk

Preheat oven to 350° F. Prepare the beets and set aside. Melt the chocolate in a double boiler; remove from heat and cool slightly. In a large bowl, lightly beat the eggs. Add the sugar, oil, vanilla, melted chocolate, and beets, stirring well after each addition. In a separate bowl, sift together the flour, baking soda, and salt and set aside. Combine the dry ingredients with the chocolate mixture and beat until just blended. Pour into a greased and floured 9-by-13-inch cake pan and bake for about 35 minutes. Remove from oven and cool before frosting.

To make the frosting, melt the chocolate in a double boiler. Remove from heat and set aside to cool. In a bowl, cream the butter, add the sugar, and beat for 5 minutes until smooth. Add the vanilla and beat thoroughly. Set aside. In a saucepan, combine the flour and ¼ cup of the milk, stirring until smooth. Gradually stir in the rest of the milk. Bring the milk to a boil over medium heat, stirring constantly. Reduce the heat to a simmer and continue stirring for 2 minutes. Remove from heat and cool quickly by placing the saucepan in a bowl of cold water, stirring all the while. Spread the frosting over the cake and refrigerate just until it sets. Garnish with flowers.
Serves 15 to 20.

Devilish Tomato Cake
with Smooth Butter Frosting

THIS SUMPTUOUS CHOCOLATE *layer cake is elegantly finished with
a satiny-smooth butter frosting. The tomatoes must be fresh, juicy,
and absolutely ripe to give this rich and distinctive cake its subtle
fruity flavor.*

      4 ounces unsweetened chocolate
      1 cup dark brown sugar
      ¼ cup milk
      2 eggs, separated
      ½ cup butter
      1 cup granulated sugar
      1¼ cups peeled, seeded, and pureed tomatoes
         (about 2 large tomatoes)
      1 teaspoon vanilla
      2 cups cake flour
      1 teaspoon baking soda
      ½ teaspoon salt
      orange or red nasturtium blossoms and leaves,
         orange or red begonia blossoms,
         or orange calendula blossoms, for garnish

SMOOTH BUTTER FROSTING
      1¼ cups butter, softened
      4 egg yolks
      ½ cup peeled, seeded, and pureed tomatoes
      1 tablespoon brandy
      ¾ cup confectioners' sugar

Preheat the oven to 350° F. In a double boiler, cook the chocolate, brown sugar, milk, and one of the egg yolks. Stir occasionally until smooth and slightly thickened. Set aside. In a large bowl, cream the butter and add the granulated sugar, beating until fluffy. Add the remaining egg yolk and beat well. Stir in the tomatoes, vanilla, and chocolate mixture and set aside. Sift together the flour, baking soda, and salt and slowly stir into the batter. In a small ceramic or glass bowl, beat the egg whites until stiff peaks form and fold into the mixture. Bake the cake in two greased and floured 9-inch cake pans for 25 to 30 minutes. Cool before removing from the pans.

To make the frosting, in a bowl cream the butter and add the egg yolks, one at a time, beating thoroughly after each addition. Stir in the tomatoes and brandy. Slowly add the confectioners' sugar and beat until smooth. Spread the frosting over the cake. Garnish with flowers. Store the cake in a cool place but not in the refrigerator.
Serves 8 to 12.

Tomato Surprise Spice Cake

THIS CAKE ACQUIRES *a mild flavor and marvelous texture from either red tomatoes or the large yellow varieties. Many people are familiar with the small pear-shaped yellow tomato, which is good for munching and tossing whole in salads, but there are also large, lush yellow tomatoes such as Golden Boy, Taxi, Lemon Boy, Jubilee, or the orange-colored Valencia. Soft, sweetened cream cheese makes a nice topping for this delightfully unconventional dessert.*

½ cup butter
1 cup brown sugar
2 eggs
¾ teaspoon grated orange zest
3 cups extra-ripe tomatoes, peeled, seeded,
    finely chopped, and drained well
½ cup raisins
½ cup chopped dates
3 cups flour
2 teaspoons baking powder
1 teaspoon baking soda
1 teaspoon ground allspice
½ teaspoon ground ginger
¼ teaspoon salt
pansies or red bee balm nestled in chamomile
    flowers, for garnish

Preheat oven to 350° F. In a large bowl, cream the butter with the sugar until fluffy. Beat in the eggs and the orange zest. Stir in the tomatoes, raisins, and dates and set aside. Sift together the flour, baking powder, baking soda, allspice, ginger, and salt. Add the dry ingredients to the tomato mixture and beat until thoroughly mixed. Pour into a greased and floured 8-by-8-inch pan and bake for about 40 to 45 minutes.
Serves 9 to 12.

Gifts from the Garden

My husband and I used to be among the post-Thanksgiving crowd,
desperately trying to find the right gifts for our ever-increasing families. Then,
four years ago, we became involved with the P-Patch Program.

With our garden yield, we lovingly prepared canned items for family and
friends. We made homemade tomato sauce from our own tomatoes, green peppers,
onions, and basil and pickles from our own cucumbers and dill. People were
impressed that we had put so much thought into their packages. Through the
years, we've added nasturtium vinegar, dried herbs, and dried sunflowers for the
bird lovers. We've found recipes for making soap with herbs and we now have a
pasta machine, so we'll see what Christmas brings to our families this year.

—A Burke Gilman gardener

Holiday Zucchini Fruitcake

GIVING A FRUIT-FILLED CAKE *as a gift during the winter holidays is an age-old tradition. Using grated zucchini to moisten the cake is a newer idea and a good one for gardeners. If you prefer dried fruit to the candied version, soak it in ¼ cup brandy to let it rehydrate before preparing the recipe. Bake your spicy gift cakes when the zucchini is plentiful in the fall to give them time to develop their rich, full flavor before the holidays.*

3 eggs	½ teaspoon freshly grated
1 cup oil	nutmeg
2 cups brown sugar	1 teaspoon salt
1 tablespoon vanilla	2 cups grated zucchini
3 cups flour	2 cups chopped walnuts
2 teaspoons baking soda	2 cups raisins
½ teaspoon baking powder	1 cup currants
2 teaspoons ground allspice	2 cups dried or candied fruit
1 teaspoon ground cloves	¼ cup brandy or rum
	(additional ¼ cup for soaking)

Preheat oven to 325° F. In a large bowl, beat the eggs, oil, and sugar until fluffy. Add the vanilla and set aside. In a separate bowl, sift together the flour, baking soda, baking powder, allspice, cloves, nutmeg, and salt. Mix the dry ingredients into the egg mixture, blending well. Stir in the zucchini, walnuts, raisins, currants, and dried or candied fruit. Pour the batter into two greased 5-by-9-inch loaf pans and bake for about 70 minutes. Test for doneness, remove from oven, and cool. Spoon one half of the brandy or rum over each loaf, allowing the liquor to soak in for about 5 minutes. Tightly wrap the fruit cakes individually and place in the refrigerator to age.
Makes two 5-by-9 loaves.

True dried currants are from black currant plants of the genus *Ribes*. Although less commonly grown in the United States than in Europe, there are many varieties available from speciality nurseries.

THE CITY GARDENER'S COOKBOOK

Tomato Jam

GIVE A PRESENT *of thick, muted-red jam that captures the flavor of those sumptuously sweet vine-ripened tomatoes. Most of us never think to use them for jam, but your ripest, sweetest tomatoes will produce a truly exotic spread delicately flavored with ginger and lemon.*

3 pounds tomatoes
6 cups sugar
juice of 1 lemon
2-inch piece of ginger, peeled and sliced

In a large kettle of boiling water, dip the tomatoes for 15 to 30 seconds to help their skins to slip off easily. Peel the tomatoes, discard the skins, and divide into two equal portions. Retaining all the juice, take half of the tomatoes and pulp them. Chop the remaining tomatoes into ¼-inch cubes. In a heavy kettle, heat the pulp and tomato pieces. In a separate saucepan, add enough water to the sugar to make a liquid and heat until all the crystals are dissolved and the syrup is clear. Pour the sugar syrup into the tomatoes, then add the lemon juice and ginger, stirring vigorously to mix all the ingredients. Cook over low heat for 2 hours, stirring frequently until the mixture is caramelized. Pour the hot jam into prepared sterilized jars and process according to the latest recommendations (see note on canning guidelines, page 204).
Makes 4 pints.

When pale, hard, and flavorless tomatoes appeared on the market, gardeners heeded the call to keep alive seeds of the flavorful old varieties. The fruit of these heirlooms can vary in color from white to pink, yellow, orange, red, and purple, and range in texture from mealy to meaty, seedy, and even hollow. In size the fruit can be anything from pea-size to gigantic, and it can have a round, pear, carrot, ruffled, egg, or heart shape. The flavors are described as winelike, nectarous, acidic, or sugar sweet. Old varieties can be dependable, with strong and sturdy growth, or sometimes a little tricky, stubborn, or even unproductive. But they all were perfect plants for someone's garden, and historically, that is reason enough to keep them. Maintaining a large, diverse, and fresh gene pool is important as well.

Hot Pepper Jelly

WITH SUCCESS IN GROWING *hot peppers such as jalapeño or red chilies comes a windfall of fruit. Besides eating them fresh in salsas, making relishes, or drying them, you can make a batch or two of jelly to enjoy all year long or to give as an exceptional gift to a friend. The rosy red jelly is customarily eaten with cream cheese and crackers, but corn bread or whole wheat tortillas are also good partners for this novel spread. The degree of hotness will depend on your peppers, but remember, as always with hot peppers, wear rubber gloves to keep the burning capsaicin out of your eyes.*

$^3/_4$ **seeded, minced red bell peppers**
$^1/_4$ **seeded, minced hot peppers**
$6^1/_2$ **cups sugar**
$1^1/_2$ **cups cider vinegar**
6 ounces liquid pectin

In a large saucepan over medium-high heat, bring the peppers, sugar, and vinegar to a rolling boil. Continue to boil for 10 minutes, then remove from heat. Add the liquid pectin and stir well. Pour the hot jelly into prepared sterilized jars and process according to the most current guidelines (see below).
Makes 4 pints.

For current canning guidelines, call the Washington State University/King County Cooperative Extension office in Seattle at (206) 296-3900.

The Department of Agriculture has a multitude of information available on subjects ranging from gardening to raising farm animals. You can receive the results of the latest findings on all aspects of food, from homegrown fruits and vegetables to orchards, beekeeping, and canning procedures. All you have to do is request the booklet of information from your Department of Agriculture's County Extension Agent, look over the listings, and pay a minimal fee to cover printing your order.

THE CITY GARDENER'S COOKBOOK

Fragrant Herb Jelly

IT MAY TAKE LONGER *to satisfy your creativity in choosing from the many herb flavors than it does to concoct a batch of these flavorful jellies. When experimenting with this already unusual jelly, we found that the combination of sweet basil, lemon basil, and a new variety, African Blue basil, worked extremely well. Mints, sages, and lemon balm are also good choices. The lovely, clear jelly can be eaten plain or mixed with cream cheese and spread on crackers, breads, scones, or bagels. Make some for yourself and tie a pretty bow on the jars you give as gifts.*

1½ cups firmly packed fresh herbs
2 cups water
2 tablespoons seasoned rice vinegar
3½ cups sugar
a pinch of salt, if desired
3 ounces liquid pectin

Wash the herbs and pat dry. With a food processor or by hand, finely mince the herbs and place in a saucepan with a tight-fitting lid. Add the water and slowly bring the mixture to a boil. Allow the mixture to boil for only 10 seconds, then remove from the heat. Cover the saucepan and let the herbs steep for 15 minutes, then strain and reserve 1½ cups of the liquid. In another saucepan mix together the measured liquid, vinegar, sugar, and salt (if used). Stir the mixture while bringing it to a hard boil. When the boil cannot be stirred down, add the pectin and continue stirring. When the mixture returns to a boil that cannot be stirred down, boil for 1 minute exactly. Remove from the heat and skim off the foam with a metal spoon. Pour the hot jelly into prepared sterilized jars, leaving a ½-inch space from the top. Seal according to latest recommendations (see note on canning guidelines, page 204). Makes 2 pints.

Garlic-Sage Vinegar

A CLEAR, GARLIC-FLAVORED VINEGAR *decorated with a floating sprig of sage makes a lovely gift and a valuable addition to any cook's pantry. Use this vinegar in recipes calling for plain vinegar and expect compliments.*

1 cup crumbled newly dried sage leaves

½ cup peeled, flattened garlic cloves

2 cups white wine vinegar

1 large fresh sage sprig, for garnish

2 whole cloves garlic

Place the crumbled sage leaves and flattened garlic in a dry, sterilized 1-quart jar. In a small saucepan, heat the vinegar almost to boiling and pour over the herbs and garlic. It should completely immerse them (if not, heat more vinegar and add to jar). Cap the jar and let it steep for a least 10 days, shaking occasionally. In a sterilized decorative bottle that is completely dry, add a fresh sage sprig and the whole garlic cloves, then pour in the strained vinegar. Cap tightly and store in a cool, dark place.
Makes 2 cups.

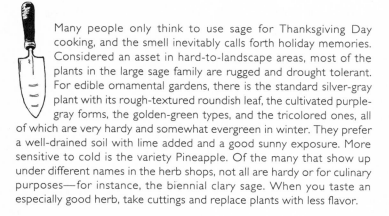

Many people only think to use sage for Thanksgiving Day cooking, and the smell inevitably calls forth holiday memories. Considered an asset in hard-to-landscape areas, most of the plants in the large sage family are rugged and drought tolerant. For edible ornamental gardens, there is the standard silver-gray plant with its rough-textured roundish leaf, the cultivated purple-gray forms, the golden-green types, and the tricolored ones, all of which are very hardy and somewhat evergreen in winter. They prefer a well-drained soil with lime added and a good sunny exposure. More sensitive to cold is the variety Pineapple. Of the many that show up under different names in the herb shops, not all are hardy or for culinary purposes—for instance, the biennial clary sage. When you taste an especially good herb, take cuttings and replace plants with less flavor.

Indian Relish

THOSE OVERABUNDANT GREEN tomatoes still hanging on the vine as the cool fall days descend upon us don't have to be neglected. Continue the tradition of sharing a garden's bounty by making gifts of this green tomato relish, a family heirloom recipe with spices of the Middle East.

12 cups finely chopped tomatoes	5 green bell peppers, finely chopped
8 cups finely chopped onions	1 red bell pepper, finely chopped
8 cups finely chopped cucumbers	1 tablespoon ground turmeric
6 tablespoons canning salt	1 teaspoon ground cinnamon
8 cups white vinegar	1 teaspoon ground cloves
6¾ cups brown sugar	
1 tablespoon yellow mustard seeds	

Using three separate bowls, place the green tomatoes in the first, the onions in the second, and the cucumber in the third. Stir in 2 tablespoons of salt in each bowl. Cover the bowls with clean cloths and let stand overnight at room temperature. The next day, drain off all the liquid from each bowl and combine the vegetables in a large kettle. Add the vinegar, sugar, and mustard seeds and stir. Bring to a boil and continue boiling for 40 minutes, stirring occasionally. Remove from heat and add the green and red peppers, turmeric, cinnamon, and cloves. Into prepared sterilized canning jars, ladle the hot relish, leaving a space of 1 inch from the top. Seal and process according to canning directions (see note on canning guidelines, page 204).
Makes 10 to 12 pints.

"Green tomato" is the term in colder climates for an unripened, immature tomato that would otherwise be red with more growing time. An exception is the heirloom variety called Evergreen, which remains green even when ripe. The flavor is full and rich, like that of the mature red tomato. Searching out heirloom seeds offers an extraordinary array of unusual vegetables.

Zucchini Relish

AFTER A SUCCESSFUL HARVEST, *make a batch of this tasty vegetable relish to serve at a grand finale feast. Bring out the flavor of grilled burgers with a juicy tomato slice, a slab of onion, and lots of relish. As you bid farewell to your guests, send them home with a gift from your pantry.*

10 cups diced zucchini	½ teaspoon freshly grated nutmeg
2 cups diced onions	
5 tablespoons canning salt	1 teaspoon ground turmeric
1 green bell pepper	1 teaspoon cornstarch
1 red bell pepper	2 teaspoons celery seeds
2½ cups vinegar	½ teaspoon freshly ground pepper
4 cups sugar	

In a large bowl, combine the diced zucchini and onions. Sprinkle in the canning salt and stir well. Cover with a clean cloth and let stand overnight at room temperature. The next day, rinse and drain the mixture twice in cold water. Set aside. Finely chop the green and red peppers and add them to the zucchini mixture. To make the syrup, combine the vinegar, sugar, nutmeg, turmeric, cornstarch, celery seeds, and pepper in a saucepan. Bring to a boil and stir until the sugar is completely dissolved. Add the vegetables and cook for 45 minutes. Pour into prepared sterilized jars and seal according to latest recommendations (see note on canning guidelines, page 204).
Makes 6 to 7 pints.

 Early in the season when the weather is cool, squash plants are slow to set fruit because the bees are not out. If you want to get a jump on the season, try hand pollinating your plants. The blossoms on the long skinny stems are the males. Cut away the petals to expose the yellow pollen grains and place them on the stigma of the female flower; it's the one with the tiny fruit at the base. When the fruit begins to swell and the flower drops off, you will know that your pollinating attempt was successful.

THE CITY GARDENER'S COOKBOOK

Dilly Green and Yellow Beans

THE AROMA AND TASTE *of dill evoke memories of glistening jars packed with the summer's bounty, quietly waiting to be opened and savored. Combine homegrown yellow beans with green ones in this classic recipe and present a colorful jar to the next friend who invites you to dinner.*

2 pounds fresh tender green beans
2 pounds fresh tender yellow beans
1³⁄₄ teaspoons crushed hot red pepper flakes
3¹⁄₂ teaspoons whole mustard seeds
14 to 21 sprigs fresh dill
7 cloves garlic
5 cups vinegar
5 cups water
¹⁄₂ cup salt

Thoroughly clean and sterilize seven 1-pint canning jars and keep hot. Wash the beans and trim, if necessary, to fit into the jars. Pack each jar with a mix of half green and half yellow beans. Add ¹⁄₄ teaspoon hot pepper, ¹⁄₂ teaspoon mustard seeds, 2 to 3 sprigs dill, and 1 clove garlic to each jar. In a saucepan, boil the vinegar, water, and salt. Pour into the jars to within ¹⁄₂ inch of the top. Seal according to latest recommendations (see note on canning guidelines, page 204).
Makes 7 pints.

 String beans, as they used to be called, had a strong fiber along the side that had to be pulled off before cooking. New strains have a less obvious "string" and will hang on the plant longer before they become fibrous. Picking the beans frequently when they are pencil-sized will give you a tender, tastier bean, a longer harvest, and an increased yield. Look for varieties that claim the ability to stay tender longer such as Golden Rocky (also available under its French name, Beau de Reaucancourt), and Blue Lake or Blue Lake–Venture. The French filet beans are not forgiving when frequent picking is neglected; they become tough and stringy.

Oven-Dried Tomatoes

FROM YOUR FIRST ENCOUNTER *with the somewhat intoxicating sweet and salty tang of these chewy dried tomatoes, you'll know that they are going to become a habit. With this recipe, you can make all the preserved tomatoes you desire and not have to rely on sunshine to dry them. Use these concentrated tomatoes in sauces, atop a warm slice of bread, or on cream cheese as an appetizer. They are also excellent in the Scones with Dried Tomatoes (page 161). A gift basket with a jar of preserved garden tomatoes never fails to please.*

> **2 pounds cherry tomatoes, halved**
> **salt to taste**
> **2 tablespoons balsamic vinegar**
> **2 teaspoons fresh basil**
> **4 cloves garlic, halved**
> **¾ cup olive oil**

Arrange the tomatoes on a baking sheet, cut side up. Sprinkle with salt and place them in a 120° F oven. Leave the oven door propped open while they dry to a shriveled and chewy texture (about 12 to 15 hours). If necessary, rearrange so they dry evenly. The ones on the edge tend to dry sooner than the center ones. Be careful not to burn them or let them become too crisp. Sprinkle with the vinegar, then drain the excess. Place in a pint jar and add the basil and garlic. Pour in the olive oil until tomatoes are covered. Store in refrigerator.
Makes 1 pint.

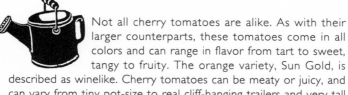

Not all cherry tomatoes are alike. As with their larger counterparts, these tomatoes come in all colors and can range in flavor from tart to sweet, tangy to fruity. The orange variety, Sun Gold, is described as winelike. Cherry tomatoes can be meaty or juicy, and can vary from tiny pot-size to real cliff-hanging trailers and very tall "mountain" climbers. Make room in next year's garden to grow a couple of different varieties.

Herb Butters

STARTING A BEAUTIFUL HERB GARDEN is a wondrous sensual experience. Raising your favorite herbs is easy; they require little attention, yet produce almost endless bouquets to gather throughout the year. Why not cultivate an array of delicious herb butters to enhance piping hot biscuits, tender scones, or divinely fresh breads? All that is required is a little softened butter and lots of imagination. Close your eyes and inhale the fragrance of just-cut herbs, then capture that same pleasure in an herb butter. Throw a fancy dinner and dazzle your guests with tiny individual cups of herb butter pressed through a pastry bag and sprinkled with minced edible flower petals. Calendula, violets, and rose petals are especially pretty. After you have discovered a particularly flavorful combination, assemble a decorative gift package of the herbs and share the recipe with others.

1 cup softened butter

2 tablespoons herbs, such as basil, marjoram, rosemary, summer savory, tarragon, thyme, or herb of your choice.

Clean and chop the herbs, then mash them into softened butter. Shape and chill to set.
Makes 1 cup.

 The ideal place to grow your favorite culinary herbs is in a sunny location outside your kitchen door, either in the ground, in window boxes, or in individual pots. Stepping stones or a narrow path meandering through your herb garden allows easy access to the plants and is both practical and attractive. Because most sun-loving herbs need well-drained, slightly alkaline soil, an addition of pumice or sand and lime is advised. Perennial herbs such as sage, rosemary, thyme, oregano, chives, and mint will give you instant "pickings" from starter plants. Annuals and biennials such as cilantro, parsley, basil, caraway, and chervil are best grown from seed. Wander through your garden often for a continuous widening of your culinary experiences.

Seasonal Menus

SPRING

ITALIAN PARSLEY PESTO WITH BABY CARROTS
CREAM OF GREENS SOUP
STUFFED SWISS CHARD LEAVES
ZESTY BEET AND POTATO SALAD
STRAWBERRY-RHUBARB CUSTARD PIE

RADISH AND CHAMPAGNE SOUP
SPRING GREENS PIE
HERBED RICE SALAD
DILLED CARROT AND PEA POD SALAD
RHUBARB COBBLER

SPINACH AND STRAWBERRY SALAD
ASPARAGUS-SPOKED CARROT AND NUT CASSEROLE
CAULIFLOWER WITH ASIAGO CHEESE
RICH CLASSIC CARROT CAKE

SUMMER

RED TOMATO TART
GRILLED CORN ON THE COB WITH FRAGRANT CILANTRO SAUCE
HERBED POTATO AND ONION BAKE
BLACKBERRY CRUMBLE

GREEN THUMB GAZPACHO
ZUCCHINI FRITTATA WITH BASIL
RED POTATO SALAD
HERBED BISCUITS WITH NASTURTIUM BUTTER
RASPBERRY MOUSSE

GARDEN ZUCCHINI SOUP
CHILLED SPAGHETTI SALAD WITH GARDEN VEGETABLES
GREEN SALAD ON THE WILD SIDE WITH BERRY VINAIGRETTE
GARDEN MUFFINS
RED RASPBERRY FLUMMERY

FALL

SESAME BEANS
GARDEN BURGERS WITH ZUCCHINI RELISH
SWEET PEPPER SLAW
DEVILISH TOMATO CAKE WITH SMOOTH BUTTER FROSTING

JACK-O'-LANTERN SOUP
PASTA WITH CILANTRO AND PUMPKIN-SEED PESTO
ITALIAN ROSEMARY AND ONION BREAD
CARROT CAKE WITH FRUIT

CURRIED BROCCOLI SOUP
COOL MINT AND CUCUMBER SALAD
MIXED VEGETABLE BHAJI
POTATOES WITH MIDDLE EASTERN SPICES
BERRY SORBET

WINTER

BEANY BROCCOLI SOUP
CHICORY SALAD WITH CURLY CRESS DRESSING
SPAGHETTI SQUASH WITH TOMATOES AND FETA CHEESE
SCONES WITH DRIED TOMATOES
SWEET WINTER SQUASH PIE

ITALIAN GREENS SOUP
WINTER ONION PIE WITH FRESH NUTMEG
TWICE-BAKED GARDEN POTATOES
BRUSSELS SPROUTS WITH WALNUT VINAIGRETTE
CHOCOLATE BEET CAKE WITH RICH CHOCOLATE FROSTING

FRESH PARSNIP SALAD
HERITAGE BEAN AND PUMPKIN STEW
CORN BREAD WITH WINTER SQUASH AND MACE
GOLDEN CARROT-OATMEAL COOKIES

A P-Patch Garden Tour

*P-Patching was a big reason I picked Seattle as a place to live.
There's something endearing about a city that frees up vacant land for
community gardens so that people can fullfill their dreams.*

— A Picardo Farmer

Admiral—The Teeniest P-Patch of All
44TH AVENUE SW AND SW SEATTLE STREET

Good land for gardeners is scarce on the northern tip of West Seattle. The Admiral P-Patch nestles in the backyard of a warehouse, amid stored lumber and saws. Seven gardening households call it home. Flowers burst out onto the alley side so that the gardeners can use all the available space for vegetables. The warehouse background is a strong contrast to the orange calendulas and stately lupines outside the fence. One older gardener spends winter making and screening compost to enrich his plot's soil. He is so successful that everyone envies his space. Another patch has an impressive assemblage of as many raspberry and blueberry plants as can fit into a 10-by-20-foot space. The P-Patch "wanna-bes" on the waiting list are pretty aggressive. They patrol the site and voice their suggestions: "That plot is getting a little weedy. Maybe it's my turn." Their voices must linger in the air until the gardeners come, for the present tenants take the hint and tend their gardens well.

Ballard—Visualize Ballard
25TH AVENUE NW AND NW 85TH STREET

If any P-Patch reflects its neighborhood, it's Ballard's, a microcosm of Scandinavian heritage. Visualize bright flower borders, tidy garden plots, a mailbox carefully lettered "Ballard, U.S.A.," a sign handmade by an Eagle Scout, a Garden of the Week award, and notices on the kiosk asking for help during a gardener's vacation. The view of Puget Sound is reminiscent of a Scandinavian vista.

Most P-Patches have resident bird populations. Interbay has pheasants; Picardo has killdeer. Ballard has parrots? Eye-catching against the background of tasseling corn, they seem incongruous, more suited to palm trees, warm climates, and pirate ships. These must undoubtedly be rare Scandinavian parrots, happy among pine trees, rainy weather, and fishing boats.

Beacon—Mixed Blessings
2528 S GRAHAM STREET

Beacon Avenue Community Garden was only one of the programs offered by the Beacon Avenue United Church of Christ, a unique place of worship for five very diverse congregations. The church entrusted the garden to the P-Patch Program in 1993 hoping that broader outreach would result in greater use of the garden. A few trouble spots needed to be resolved, among them, acid soil and shade from the neighbor's pine tree.

The famous 1993 Inaugural Day storm brought mixed blessings. It blew in a time of change and hope, and it promptly took care of the shade problem. The tree shattered and fell . . . into the garden. The Conservation Corps came to the rescue and removed the tree, giving the garden full sunlight . . . and ending the acidifying pine needles. Then Cedar Grove Compost came to the rescue with truckloads of compost. Now there is good soil, too. Miracles happen, especially when five congregations and lots of gardeners work together.

Belltown—Making the Dream Reality
ELLIOTT AVENUE AND VINE STREET

When the P-Patch 20th Anniversary Time Capsule was buried in July 1993, soil samples were included from all 30 P-Patch sites. Some people thought the Belltown canister was empty. Granted, it had no soil, but it was full of the dream to come. The dream had been growing for four years, and although ground break-ing was still ahead, the Friends of a Belltown P-Patch had already achieved wonders. They had convinced the city to buy the site for open space preservation and to build a community garden. It might not have been too hard to save as open space the only unpaved lot remaining in the whole Denny Regrade. But considering the process for nomination, the public meetings, and the competition for funds, the feat is nothing short of a miracle.

The Friends of a Belltown P-Patch are believers in miracles. The garden-to-be is now home to the homeless, a focal point of a neighborhood working for social equity, a testament to the essential connection to the earth. The garden design strongly reflects Belltown and its artists, condo dwellers, light industries, social services, and green guerrillas. Urban green guerrilla tactics could describe the actions of the Friends: chalk sidewalk drawings preceding public hearings, weekend billboard reclamations, plywood sunflowers, bee bonnets, and courtship of the media. All of these are stones on the path to the garden. Now that the stones have been laid, the garden will soon follow.

Burke Gilman Place—Making Soil
SANDPOINT WAY NE AND NE 52ND STREET

Burke Gilman P-Patch is a wet site. Each spring the gardeners wait for the soil to dry so they can add lots of leaf mold and compost. With wheelbarrows and shovels they work hard to change dirt into soil, magically transforming bricklike clay into product-ive earth. The garden has space for kids too (and there are more of them than adults in the neighbor-hood). One section of the garden is set aside in little 2-by-3-foot beds for children, enough room to plant one tomato plant, a sunflower, a pumpkin, a small stand of corn. The younger gardeners at Burke Gilman are just learning that food comes from plants. For other residents, recent immigrants from the Soviet bloc, the P-Patch provides a chance to garden again; they are anxious to plant in a space they can call their own. Sorrel, dill, beets, and cabbages form a productive patchwork and the foundation of many meals.

Cherry Street—A Cheerful Conclusion?
29TH AVENUE AND E CHERRY STREET

A story looking for a sweet conclusion, this is how one could describe the Cherry Street P-Patch. During the 1980s this little garden was tended by small hands from the nearby Girls Club. Over the years the girls turned to other interests, and Homer took on larger pieces of the garden to grow fresh greens for his elderly neighbors. In 1992 the owners offered the lot for P-Patch use and many families joined Homer in caring for the site, "growing their own" and trying to beautify the garden. It became a cheerful place.

But the owners have not decided whether to sell the lot for housing or to make it a permanent garden; they will choose soon. The gardeners have pledged to improve the site with a new fence, permanent compost bins, an arbor entry, flowered borders, a toolshed, anything it takes. Their vision is to make the garden the best neighbor, if only they can secure the site. So today's challenge is to help the gardeners and the owners grow together. When ownership is resolved, we hope the garden will be cheerful Cherry.

Colman Park—A Morning Garden
32ND AVENUE S AND S GRAND STREET

The heaviness of the air, laden with blackberries, lures the whole neighborhood into Colman Park. Summer is at its peak. Wander through and enjoy the views: each terrace reflects a different gardening style. One gardener experiments with exotics— saffron crocus, water chestnuts, wine grapes and tries heavy mulch instead of weeding. Down one level is a highly productive, meticulously weeded garden displaying the latest techniques—floating row covers, trellises, cloches, and weed barriers. Just a little way down the hill is the herb specialist, followed by the flower devotee; then comes an Asian garden filled with squashes of all colors, and a midwestern garden with straight rows of corn. Colman Park faces east, toward Lake Washington, and wakes early. The birds sing at the first pink light; neighbors walk their "leashed" dogs. The dew rests lightly, and by late afternoon the blackberries call out to be eaten.

Delridge—Sharing the Space
DELRIDGE WAY SW AND SW PUGET BOULEVARD

Quietly, through the grass, the little black garter snake escapes. He's frightened of the noisy weed whackers cutting the grassy slope near his home. His family has lived here for years in peace, taking good care of the garden. He's observed the gardeners: Giuseppina planting radicchio, Yang harvesting cilantro, Gerhardt picking leeks. The snake has watched as they've built compost bins, mowed grass, and attacked weeds. He's wondering why they had to be so noisy. He's always preferred their softer sounds: turning soil, harvesting warm tomatoes, and humming while cutting cosmos. Sunday morning hymns from the church next door are nice, too. But he decides that if he has to share his home, these people aren't so bad as neighbors.

Eastlake—A Valentine P-Patch

2900 FAIRVIEW AVENUE E

 Neighbors met at the site on February 14 to uncover a lost love. All they needed to do was cut the blackberries away and they would have a garden. Attacking with only a few sets of hand pruners proved difficult, but determined work party crews minced them. Hidden below were the unexpected: dead car parts, appliances, garbage, and disintegrating tangles of colored threads knotted with roots and plants—old carpets. Huge loads of moldy carpets were crammed into a Volkswagen and hauled to the dump. At last they were ready: they tilled the garden and built raised beds, compost bins, and a bench for lunching and viewing Lake Union. The produce started rolling in. First were the radishes, red as a Valentine, which were accepted gratefully for the first spring salad potluck.

The gardeners thought they were safe. Who would bother them, nestled among the blackberries, on a street right-of-way too steep to develop? But first a building was to be demolished, and access could only be gained through the garden. "A road," said some. "A garden," said others. After a hard-fought battle, three plots were lost to the road, but the garden was saved. Then they were in the shadow of a major development; access would require paving the garden. The dedicated Eastlake Community Council sprang into action. The Save the Garden committee developed into the Fairview–Olmsted Park Commission, which stalwartly worked to save the P-Patch and proposed that the land adjacent be purchased for a park. Soon the Eastlake P-Patch will be surrounded by a new park, and the red radishes will flourish.

Estelle Street P-Patch—Trading Blackberries for Gardens
S ESTELLE STREET AND WETMORE PLACE S

As the third-grade class visited the mayor's office, one of the children complained that his walking route to school was scary. There were people hiding in the blackberries, dealing drugs. And so South East Effective Development started to clear the street right-of-way. Their landscape design required frequent care. At the same time, residents of the adjacent tenant-managed apartment wanted a garden. The two ideas blended into one at the Estelle Street P-Patch. In a few short weeks SEED crews built a garden that reflected the gardeners' needs. The neighbors, who had gardened nearby until their gardens were lost to development, were delighted to regain space for their greens, mustards, and onions.

The gardens blossomed with children and adults, tomatoes and garlic, basil and cilantro.

The scary place became safe, and the heady smells and bright colors were a magnet for visitors.

Now the only drugs are in the occasional opium poppy, grown from seeds from the past.

Evanston—There Is Always the Garden
EVANSTON AVENUE N AND N 102ND STREET

Evanston P-Patch is a peaceful refuge for busy people. The seniors come in the mornings; workers drop in at lunchtime or on the way home; and families come in the evenings. There is often someone enjoying the solitude, losing the day's worries by working in the soil, picking some of Helen's scarlet poppies, blue bachelor's buttons, or golden calendulas near her sign saying "Pick some of these to enjoy."

The P-Patch garden is filled with memories of past gardeners: white-haired gentlemen like meticulous old Bruno, and John, who carefully cut the grass and painted the shed. Their legacy lives on: even though new gardeners arrive every year, they learn techniques passed down from the veterans. At Evanston, there is always the garden to bring peace, solace, and friendship.

Ferdinand—Growing Families
COLUMBIA DRIVE S AND S FERDINAND STREET

High on Beacon Hill, on the freezing last Saturday in February, an annual ritual takes place. Pouring from their cars, with children strapped on their backs, come the gardeners. Refugees from Southeast Asia, these women want to sign up for their little vegetable gardens and plant seeds from home. Each year we greet them, gratified to recognize the same happy faces, see the children bigger than last year, meet the new babies in their colorful costumes. In a few short weeks the site will be transformed from a sleeping winter garden into an abundance of greens. Small children will scamper between the row as their mothers harvest bitter melon, *gai lohn*, *gai choy*, yard-long beans, and fragrant cilantro. But today the gardens are at rest, and only the native costumes and familiar smiles lend warmth to the grayness.

Good Shepherd—Home of True Conversions
BAGLEY AVENUE N AND N 47TH STREET

Thwack! Sproing! Thwack! Sproing! Tennis sounds reverberated around the site. Then Bang! Thud! Bang! Thud! Bulldozers broke up the old concrete courts. Laugh! Sigh! Dig, dig, dig! These are the sounds you hear now at the Good Shepherd P-Patch.

Many years ago the Good Shepherd Center was a home for girls. In the mid-1970s the Sisters of the Good Shepherd sold the site to the city for a new Wallingford park. The Wallingford Community Council and many neighborhood activists were involved in site design. They wanted their park to reflect the neighborhood's soul and to ensure that an urban agricultural center would be part of the new development. Their visions were grand; they included a greenhouse, a teaching center, and a community garden. We can thank them for their foresight, for all of those activities come together at Good Shepherd every day. The magical Tilth Garden, greenhouse, and teaching center complement the P-Patches nestled nearby. You can hear the laughter of discovery from the Tilth Pee Wee Children's Garden. The surrounding park abounds with activities, silent Tai Chi sessions, noisier weddings, picnics, and chamber music in the gazebo. And the voices of gardeners sharing tall vegetable tales bounce off the Good Shepherd Center walls.

Holly Park—Growing a Garden
40TH AVENUE S AND WEBSTER COURT

Since it was late May, the Webster Court garden sprouted quickly. Matching grant funds with sweat equity, neighbors and volunteers plunged into the project. With English, Vietnamese, and Cambodian words flying, somehow everyone understood what needed to be done. Measurements were shown with two hands, "This far." Everyone dug in. Into the rock-hard soil went the fence-post holes and the trench for the water line. Goat manure, lime, and fertilizer were quickly mixed in. The painting team followed on the heels of the fence builders; the wire stretchers followed the painters. Almost before the paint was dry, the gardens were planted. These people clearly were accustomed to hard work. Ton had built temples in Cambodia; Heng Hay had a network of friends to lend tools. It seemed important to build quickly—it was time to put the seeds in the ground!

Holly Park P-Patch was built not only to provide food and friendship. It is a garden with bigger goals: driving out drug dealing, building trust among neighbors, and helping non-English-speaking people take an active part in their community.

Interbay—One Hundred Gardeners Strong
15TH AVENUE W AND W ARMOUR STREET

In the mid-1970s, when community gardens started in Seattle, the Interbay P-Patchers began gardening on a thick clay cap of an old landfill between the neighborhoods of Queen Anne and Magnolia. The site was large, in the middle of a wasteland. Phantom dumping was common but so were pheasants, quail, and songbirds. The sound of the rail yard was always near. The drainage on the clay was poor, but the gardeners were a hearty bunch, hauling mountains of organic materials to build up the soil.

Then came the 1980s. A golf course was planned for "their" land. The gardeners, 100 strong, asked the city fathers to save an acre for their gardens when the golf course was eventually built. "Yes," the city fathers said, "just don't bring us any more zucchini, please!" With the 1990s, visions of golf came ever nearer. The plans were drawn, and the gardens had to move. Bulldozers invaded the peaceful turf of Interbay as 100 gardeners with an army of wheelbarrows moved precious soil and plants, lovingly developed over the years, to the new Interbay P-Patch. Garden slaves, garden gnomes, garden heroes and heroines, garden fairies worked all through the summer of 1992 to make themselves a new home. A toolshed, always dreamed of, became a reality. A Food Bank collection station was built to hold donations to those in need. Real compost bins graced the site. Fruit trees formed the foundation of an urban orchard.

Today the Interbay P-Patch is a place of peace, beauty, and productivity, designed and built by the many who cared passionately about preserving a place to grow food and friends! The year 2000 is not far away. Will this be a true Seattle garden? Will lattes be sold from the toolshed?

Jackson Park—Where the Living Is Easy
10TH AVENUE NE AND NE 133RD STREET

There's silver-haired Margaret, all in purple, proudly staking up blue delphiniums and goldenrod that spill from her flower beds. Bob's scheming up a project to add trellises to the raised beds; Lee's mowing the back 40; and Glenn's orchestrating as his friends from the seniors' residence harvest shiny-ripe strawberries for the evening's shortcake: summertime at Jackson Park and the living is truly easy.

They're all hoping that Randy will come by. For Randy, gardening equals basil, a whole 10-by-40-foot plot of it, perhaps too much even for Randy. They are lucky: he comes, and conversations, flowers, vegetables, and, most importantly, basil flow throughout the garden. The spicy basil scent lingers in the evening air long after the gardeners have gone home.

Judkins—The Tradition of Marbles
24TH AVENUE S AND S NORMAN STREET

Six truckloads of stuff were hauled away before ground level appeared. All kinds of treasures were hiding under the blackberries: overstuffed couches, a blue plastic horse, and marbles. The couches went directly to the dump; the horse took up residency with an office plant; and the marbles rolled around on the P-Patch car's dashboard.

Gardeners moved into Judkins. Pink cleome tutus danced in the breeze above chunks of concrete. Rocks bred like rabbits. Judkins lived as a garden of contrasts. Lovingly tended plots snuggled up to the encroaching blackberries; rocks enclosed areas of sifted soil; and flowers shared the limelight with vegetables.

The gardeners continue to discover marbles sparkling in the soil, winking cat's-eyes and aggies telling stories of the past: "This land belonged to others, and it will belong to others again. New gardeners will take your place and dream of future harvests." At Judkins P-Patch the fragile thread of a community garden has been firmly woven into the soil and will continue to surface as reliably as those shining marbles.

Marion—Gifts from Other P-Patches
24TH AVENUE E AND E MARION STREET

The lot was overgrown. "Smooth-tailed squirrels" lived there; clearly too much flora and fauna of the wrong kind inhabited the place. The neighborhood was ready when the owner offered the site for P-Patching. They wanted flowers, vegetables, and a fence.

After clearing, hauling manure, and rototilling, it was time for fence building. Roger and Brian, two volunteer carpenters from other P-Patches, miraculously appeared to teach Conservation Corps members the intricacies of fence building. The transfer of skills was terrific, and corps members were justly proud of "their" fence. They even gathered used brick and inlaid an entry path. More gifts arrived: perennial flowers for the street side from

Richard, planting help from Master Gardener Krizten, and a demonstration garden plot from Connie at the Seattle Food Garden Project. It took lots of work, by many hands, but the flora and fauna have been replaced by far more desirable species.

Mt. Baker—Colors at Their Best
29TH AVENUE S AND S GRAND STREET

Mt. Baker P-Patch boasts the best view in the city, and on a clear day you can see . . . downtown. A closer look at the garden reflects a view of the whole city. There are heady, fragrant cilantro patches, scarlet peppers, rows of silky corn, occasional opium poppies, and frequent basketballs from the adjacent court, all reflecting Mt. Baker P-Patch as a busy, culturally diverse neighborhood.

Mt. Baker also boasts the most colorful garden signs in the city. "Water Wisely," "Take Your Garbage Home," and "Compostables Only" signs are strategically placed around the site. Joyce, the site coordinator, painted the eye-catching signs of blue, green, yellow and magenta as gentle reminders of how those who share the site can make it better. Brooke, the 8-foot scarecrow made by a local artist and young assistants, oversees the garden. Her purple, hot pink, and chartreuse costume is perfect garden attire for Mt. Baker. Her hot jewels swinging in the breeze speak of freedom and vegetables for all.

Phinney Ridge—Billy Goat's Bluff
3RD AVENUE NW AND NW 60TH STREET

The slope was so steep we almost rolled off the hill. "So that's what a 30-percent grade looks like." We were standing on the top of Phinney Ridge looking toward the sound as Eldon and Claire talked of their dream of turning this derelict street right-of-way into the Hanging Gardens of Phinney Ridge. Their dream took our breath away and made us think of mountain goats.

Eldon and Claire worked with their community to secure grant funding for materials to tame the neighborhood four-wheel-drive raceway and turn it into a garden. Clearing the site was hard enough, but then construction day dawned. Three hundred forty timbers arrived on a flatbed truck, 100 pounds apiece. Volunteers unloaded timbers, carved terraces into the hillside, built raised garden beds, and made fast friendships. Finally 1,200 volunteer hours later, after a winter's rest and renewed spring energy, they finished. The garden beds were filled with soil and truckloads of goat manure. The vegetables fairly sprang out of the soil.

The garden was dedicated in August 1991 as the Phinney Ridge P-Patch, but it is affectionately known as Billy Goat's Bluff because of the goat manure and the fact that only mountain goats could garden on such a steep slope. The site is a testament to what people of vision, dedication, and energy can do together. A plaque on 3rd Avenue NW is dedicated to Eldon, who never got to see his dream completed. Bob and Kathryn were awarded commendations from Mayor Rice for their pivotal roles in completing the garden. Now four-wheel drives no longer break the nighttime stillness. Can you hear the zucchini growing?

Picardo Farm—Celebrate Soil!
26TH AVENUE NE AND NE 82ND STREET

There's dirt and then there's soil. Picardo Farm P-Patch, the original and biggest garden, is the home of Seattle's best soil. If one could be eloquent about soil, this garden would provide the inspiration. Rich, black, peaty, sucking with moisture in the spring, powdery dry for digging potatoes, so full of life that crops (and, alas, weeds) spring out of the ground at alarming rates.

Picardo's size amazes. You can get lost among the towering corn and sunflowers. Two hundred and fifty gardeners share this paradise. They work diligently composting, combating comfrey, and making friends. We know of at least three marriages that started over a row of peas.

Picardo Farm is unique. As the original Seattle community garden, it has the longest-term gardeners, dedicated people who for years have tilled the soil and cultivated the program. It is also unique in having the longest quack grass roots in the city, the greatest number of comfrey plants per acre, and the most numerous slugs in the universe. Each spring before plowing, the killdeer nest on the bare soil. Like David taking on Goliath, they try to lure the tractors away from their nests with calls and broken-wing tactics. Each spring some gardeners as they receive their plots also become foster parents to the baby killdeer.

For the 20th anniversary celebration, instead of the usual tractors, six teams of enormous draft horses plowed the site. Imagine the steam rising from the horses' nostrils as they strained to turn the heavy, wet soil, their hooves thudding through the earth as the plow turned stripes of black soil and hid the green weeds of winter. Imagine the teams working, while the spectators stood hushed in awe. It was a day of return to the past and to the wonder of nature. One could hear the soil say, "Plant seeds here."

Pinehurst—A Real Victory Garden
12TH AVENUE NE AND NE 115TH STREET

The gardeners at Pinehurst P-Patch had always prided themselves on the beauty of their abundant garden: the red lettuce planted in a checkerboard with the green, the communal herb bed bordered in colorful flowers, the overflowing loads of vegetables ready for Neighbors in Need, the neatly barked paths, the freshly turned compost. They worked closely to build what is the best small community garden in the nation, according to the judges of the American Community Gardening Association.

Then, one summer, the owners of the site decided to sell to a developer. The bulldozers stood ready to level this prize-winning garden. Blind optimism, flavored with large doses of hard work, petitions, TV stories, baskets of vegetables delivered with letters of appeal—all these played a part in saving the garden. The developer deeded one lot to the P-Patch Advisory Council, and it became the first owned and permanently protected garden. Pinehurst gardeners revel in the knowledge that the garden is forever, maybe not for themselves, but for all the gardeners who will be able to "grow their own" for many years to come. Today it provides a quiet haven where visitors eat lunch nestled among the flowers, children visit from the nearby school, and a host of scarecrows watches over the bees buzzing between the berries. Peace reigns in the P-Patch.

Rainier Vista—Introductions

4400 TAMARACK DRIVE S

New gardens bring their own rewards as people get to know one another. Rainier Vista is no exception, with gardeners whose roots are often southern or midwestern. The crop choices also are rooted in other regions: peppers, okra, and eggplant. Bea introduced salsify, or oyster plant. With its mild oyster flavor, cooked, mashed salsify can be made into patties, breaded, and fried somewhat like oysters. Eating salsify, however, does not have the same effect as slurping raw oysters on the beach. Trust me.

Rainier Vista's garden is full of challenges: weeds and slugs love to congregate near the retaining boards on the slope. Some aspiring gardeners use wheelchairs. That challenge was easy to solve: accessible raised beds were installed so that all could have the opportunity to garden. The problem of slugs and weeds has yet to be solved.

Ravenna—The Secret Garden

5200 RAVENNA AVENUE NE

Tucked into a pedestrian street right-of-way, behind a row of plum trees, lies a little jewel, Ravenna's secret garden. In the late 1970s the site was an overgrown hillside with a trampled path. The Seattle Engineering Department planned to build a stairway on the steepest part of the site and accepted the challenge of including a P-Patch on the flatter part. A beautifully designed, fully landscaped garden with space for 11 gardening households opened in 1981. The gardeners quickly outgrew their plots and adopted the hillside, naturalizing it with daffodils and tulips.

Ten peaceful years of tomatoes later, an access roadway for an adjacent development threatened to pave over the P-Patch, but the whole neighborhood galvanized behind the tomatoes, and the gardeners. Today tomatoes, not asphalt, grace the secret garden.

THE CITY GARDENER'S COOKBOOK

Republican—Affairs of the Heart
20TH AVENUE E AND E REPUBLICAN STREET

Capitol Hill is one of Seattle's most densely populated, politically and philosophically diverse neighborhoods, and the P-Patch on Republican Street is the only community garden serving the area. With apartments looming around it, there is space for only 13 households and the waiting list is forever.

The gardeners love their small site. Compost bins hunker down in the corner, quietly producing humus. A fragrant rambling rose crawls over the back fence. The entry arbor is flanked by carefully tended flowers. These gardeners lavish time on their space. Norm's wife, a divorce counselor, appreciates that his only love affair is with the garden. He comes home with a full heart and fresh greens for supper; he is one of the lucky ones to have a space. In a neighborhood teeming with people, Republican P-Patch clearly has too few spaces for too many would-be gardeners. The P-Patch Advisory Council has established a donor fund to acquire more land for Capitol Hill gardeners. In order to be fair, they are looking for land on Democrat Street.

Sandpoint—The Country Club
SANDPOINT WAY NE AND NE 70TH STREET

On any sunny summer Sunday they might be there, sitting in lawn chairs, supervising the corn growing, and reading the morning paper. Sandpoint P-Patch invites people to stay awhile, so they bring deck chairs, plant lots of roses, and gather flavorful blackberries to nibble for brunch. The garden is almost hidden among the sweetly scented cottonwood trees and is graced with birds nesting in the apple and pear trees of a homesteader's orchard. Which kind of pie should we bake, blackberry or apple?

Snoqualmie—High on a Hill
13TH AVENUE S AND S SNOQUALMIE STREET

Firmly planted on the crest of Beacon Hill, with a refreshing breeze blowing through the springtime mustard blossoms, is the Snoqualmie P-Patch. The Seattle Food Garden Project's demonstration garden makes this site an important teaching garden for Seattle's newest immigrants. At his weekly Garden Hour Yao Fou encourages gardeners to try new methods for an abundance of *ghee*, yard-long beans, and bitter melon. He stresses watering in summer, planting crops in succession, and trapping slugs. His methods are proven in his demonstration plot, which bursts with gorgeous vegetables.

Thistle—The Southend Farm
MARTIN LUTHER KING JR. WAY AND S CLOVERDALE STREET

Started in the mid-1970s, the Thistle P-Patch had become a sorry spot by the early 1980s. Forty garden plots, many unused and weedy, sat on some of the richest bottomland around. The garden was rediscovered when numerous refugee families moved from Southeast Asia to southeast Seattle. They brought with them wonderful gardening skills, unusual tools, a willingness to work incredibly hard, and seeds! We heard, "What is that plant?" and "How do you eat it?"

A visit to Thistle is like a tour of the world. Italian tomatoes grow side by side with oriental *shizo*. Midwestern row gardens adjoin widely broadcast raised beds of greens. Koreans plant next to Vietnamese, Italians, Cambodians—all Americans now. Seniors garden next to moms with babies on their backs. Early spring is the best time to visit, when the black soil, freshly turned, contrasts with the succulent greens.

Thistle P-Patch has grown over the years. A 1990 grant from Puget Consumers Co-op paid for materials to expand the water system and till more land. From the original 40 plots, the site is now over an acre, on which more than 125 families produce food. From gardeners working hard to feed their families we hear, "Oh, just a little space to grow one more row of peas," or, "My sister's family just came here and they really need a garden."

University District—A Garden for Everyone
8TH AVENUE NE AND NE 40TH STREET

The University District P-Patch garden paths are the most popular shortcut in the district. In one of the city's most heavily traveled neighborhoods, many people walk through the garden to learn what's new in the vegetable kingdom, vicariously participate in nature's seasons, and stop to smell the flowers. Passersby appreciate the blossoms and herbs spilling onto the sidewalks; they marvel at the dwarf apple trees in the parking strips. Even bus passengers on the interstate freeway can view the garden and delight in the wintertime messages of sawdust on the bare soil: "Peas on Earth," "Happy Holidays," or "I Love My P-Patch." The University District P-Patch reaches out to all of Seattle.

University Heights—Patchworks
UNIVERSITY WAY NE AND NE 50TH STREET

The P-Patch built the fastest is at the University Heights Center for the Community. A sign on the fence lured in volunteers, who arrived at the same time as the load of supplies. The site was quickly cleared, and by the end of the first day each member of the construction crew took a rest in an empty kid-sized raised bed. Six beds with six tired bodies; they did make a funny sight, almost as if they'd found their final resting spots! Week two saw construction of the larger raised beds and the arrival of leaf compost, topsoil, organic soil amendments, and three mountains of wood chips. It seemed as if everything came in 10-yard loads. Ten yards can fill a lot of wheel-barrows many times. Anxious gardeners planted even before the fence was finished. The gate with the yellow sunburst rays was the final touch.

With four school groups using the site, the first crops yielded wonders. Children with shining eyes discovered that pole beans all climb by spiraling in the same direction, that zucchini plants have prickly leaves and too many zucchini, and that fresh carrots right out of the ground are the sweetest! Patchworks is a tiny site with lots of tiny gardeners, each one growing nearly as fast as the plants.

INDEX

THE CITY GARDENER'S COOKBOOK